COLLINS PO

FINDING A JOB

Louise Bostock Lang

HarperCollins*Publishers*

HarperCollins Publishers
P.O. Box, Glasgow G4 0NB

First published 1996

Reprint 10 9 8 7 6 5 4 3 2 1 0

© HarperCollins Publishers 1996

ISBN 0 00 470977 2

Typeset by Eye to Eye Publishing & Design, London

Printed and bound in Great Britain by Caledonian International
Book Manufacturing Ltd, Glasgow, G64

CONTENTS

Introduction 5

1 Bargaining power 7
2 Planning the search 27
3 Avenues to work 48
4 Getting through 75
5 Interviews and meetings 129
6 Post-interview activities 166
7 Advice for women returners 178
8 Advice for older workers 185
9 Contract and home working 193
10 Looking for work abroad 201

A–Z of work-related terms 209
List of occupations 222
Index 238

INTRODUCTION

Collins Pocket Reference Finding a Job is a complete guide to job-hunting. It covers every aspect of the search for work from effective organization to negotiating terms when a job is offered. Subjects include: creating a network of contacts so that you hear about jobs *before* they are advertised; making opportunities for yourself and staying in work when others are being made redundant; how to draft a winning CV and how to make successful job applications that reflect your special qualities; where to look for job opportunities; preparing for interviews and coping with different interview styles; identifying an employer's needs and persuading the employer that you alone can fill those needs; overcoming problems such as handicaps, periods of unemployment, lack of experience or qualifications. It also gives invaluable advice on becoming self-employed and working at home, and for special groups such as older people, women returning to work or joining the workforce later in life and those looking for work abroad.

A large part of the book is devoted to helping the job-hunter understand his or her own skills, experience and temperament, so that these can be displayed to the recruiter in the best light. The other side of this coin is understanding what the recruiter is looking for, and how the company's needs are explained in advertisements and interviews, and so space has been given to interpreting advertisements and finding out in advance about both the target company and the job in question. The book also helps the job-hunter to choose a career path that will be rewarding and successful, and encourages job-seekers to have the confidence to change careers if it seems that the chosen path may have become unsatisfactory or insecure.

In the second part of the book are a glossary of terms related to job-hunting, training and the world of work in general, and a classified list of more than 600 jobs to provide inspiration for school-leavers thinking of embarking on their new career, but also for anyone interested in changing their course at any time of life.

In these days of redundancy, unemployment and increasing competitiveness for secure positions, *Collins Pocket Reference Finding a Job* teaches job-hunters all the skills needed for a successful search and for maintaining a fulfilling and successful career path throughout their lives.

BARGAINING POWER

*'Perfect freedom is reserved for the man who lives by his
own work and in that work does what he wants to do.'*
R.G. Collingwood (1889–1943)

It's no secret any longer. The job-for-life as our parents and
grandparents knew it is extinct. No longer can we expect to be
employed full-time by a single company throughout our lives,
with a predictable promotion ladder to climb and to measure
our success by, and with all sorts of benefits and company
perks thrown in. Gone too is the feeling of community when a
single large employer provides a livelihood for the entire area.

The present offers a very different picture: young people
unable to find steady work after they leave school or graduate
from college or university; older people forced to change jobs
many times during their working lives, no longer able to count
on a steady increase in affluence as they become more
experienced; women returning to the world of work after
periods bringing up a family; lone parents juggling part-time
jobs with childcare.

And the future, as now being predicted by a handful of social
analysts, is almost unrecognizable: the majority of workers,
they say, will be employed on a short contract basis, moving
from project to project, company to company, as the need
arises, fulfilling one, two or maybe even more functions in
different parts of their working lives, benefitting from the

variety of jobs but losing the security of being in 'permanent' employment. Companies will, say the analysts, employ only a handful of core staff, mainly in administrative functions. They will buy in other skills and services only when needed. Indeed, we are already seeing 'outplacement' on a large scale in many of the world's largest companies, and along with that change, the appearance of thousands of small companies operating with one or two permanent staff only.

If we are to believe this future scenario (and there is compelling evidence that we should), a huge change in attitude towards work must take place. Workers will need to view themselves as providers of a service to customers and clients (the 'employers'). They will have to identify what it is that the employer needs and they will have to market their 'product' in such a way that it is 'bought' in preference to the services of others. Workers will need to manage their careers on a day-to-day basis. Job-search skills will be in use every week rather than from time to time. Workers will spend more time looking for new 'employers' or customers, and a great deal more time enhancing and packaging their skills.

The concept of the 'career' as an unbroken journey towards a particular goal is officially bankrupt. We need to find other ways in which to define our life's work and other ways in which to define success. Young people can no longer decide what subjects to study at the age of 14, 16 or 18, knowing that this decision will set them on a straight path towards a particular career goal. We will need to be able to identify in ourselves a wide range of skills, experience, qualifications and specialist knowledge, and view these assets in terms of what is needed by those who are going to be paying us.

If the world of work is a market place in which the workers' services are exchanged for something else (in most cases, money), the first step towards that market place is to define what we have to offer, and what we want in return.

The employment market of the future sounds terrifying: few permanent jobs, less security, no company benefits, the constant need to search for work, no career structure, no way to measure success. But, looked at a little more closely, the changes could bring some unexpected benefits:

- More variety in the work you find yourself being paid to do, and in the types of employer you do it for.
- More flexibility: you could decide to do a part-time job to support yourself while you do something infinitely more interesting with the rest of your time.
- No more problems over those awkward patches of so-called unemployment on your curriculum vitae (CV), no more worries about deciding to change horses in mid-stream and undertake a completely different kind of work – most people will be doing it.
- More flexibility in work patterns: using new technology, many jobs can now be carried out at home, enabling parents to look after young children, and those who are tired of the daily commute to throw away their season tickets.

While the problems of financial insecurity and poverty brought about by the extinction of so many jobs should not be underestimated, there are many advantages to the changes taking place that could improve many people's lives dramatically.

To benefit from the changes, each of us must be constantly assessing and re-assessing our 'product': our practical skills, specialist knowledge, hands-on experience and academic strengths. At the same time we must learn to define for ourselves what kind of life we want to lead, and what we want to have achieved at the end of it. This is extremely hard work, particularly if we are the kind of people who define success by job title and salary level, and go to work day by day through habit alone.

We should subject ourselves to a rigorous assessment, not only when starting to look for work but also at regular intervals throughout our workings lives. How can we hope to convince an employer to buy our services when we don't know what those services consist of? Furthermore, as day follows day we all change. Things happen to us and may sometimes change our views on what we want to do with our lives. We learn things about the world and about ourselves which broaden our horizons and show us what we are missing. What might have seemed like the perfect career path at the age of 18, could, as early as 28 be a road to misery. Taking stock of these changes in ourselves and in our knowledge of the world enables us to be prepared to recognize opportunities and grasp them firmly when they present themselves.

At the same time, what you learn from your self-assessment should help to increase your confidence. If you are a parent who has spent the last 10 years bringing up a family, it must be difficult to raise the confidence to be certain that you have skills someone wants to buy, and if you have worked all your life for one employer (the Armed Forces, perhaps), it may be a confidence-booster to find out that you have skills that will be valued in the outside world.

While it is hard work, self-assessment should also be enjoyable. After all, everybody's favourite subject is him- or herself, and self-assessment gives you the opportunity to think about yourself in depth for quite some time!

The process of self-assessment will also give you plenty of material when writing your CV and filling out application forms (see pages 75–128). So it is not only enjoyable but doubly useful.

Preparation

In order to carry out a full assessment, you will need:

- A number of large pieces of blank paper (a large, cheap sketchbook, or a scrap book could be made to work) and a pencil and rubber.
- Copies of previous CVs, if any, or copies of any documents that will help you recall your education and past work experience in detail.

The process of self-assessment is essentially one of making lists of words that apply to yourself and then of arranging the words so that they form some sort of pattern, leading to a number of conclusions about your aptitudes, goals and methods of working. This process will not necessarily lead to a shortlist of jobs that you are equipped to do, chiselled in stone. In fact, the aim is completely the opposite. It is to define a wide range of roles in which you would perform well and in which you would be contented and satisfied (emotionally and financially). It should prompt your own imagination to develop a scenario (or two, or even more scenarios) in which you can see yourself successfully selling your skills, and leading a lifestyle that is in keeping with your needs and temperament.

Take a single sheet of paper for each of the 'area' headings listed below. Under each heading you will write a list of words, phrases or full sentences that describe various attributes, experiences, skills or desires that you believe yourself to have. You may like to read through to the end of this chapter before you start so that you can assess the time you need to do this, and see the whole process from start to finish.

It is not necessary to complete one 'area' before you start the next. Indeed, things will probably occur to you as you work through different areas, and you should add them to previous lists as necessary. Painters are taught to work across the whole canvas at once when producing a painting, and, although your canvas is fragmented into separate pieces, you should be prepared for ideas to arise in one area when you are working on another. If they do, write them down in the relevant area at once, before you forget what they are.

Area 1: Work experience and job-related skills

- Write down each of your jobs, giving dates, location (town only), the name of the company and of your immediate superior. For each one, give job title only. Include every job you have ever been paid to do. Remember to include mowing lawns for Bob-a-Job week, baby-sitting a young sibling, Saturday jobs, paper rounds, evening work and moonlighting.

- In another part of your sheet of paper, start to make a list of the tasks you fulfilled. This time you will need to use full sentences. Each sentence should include the following elements: Who? (I) Did what? (wrote a report) Why? (to analyse the staffing problems on the project). Try to add some sort of success rating, and give hard figures if you can:

'I increased sales in my region 10% in less than six months, from a turnover of £40,000 to one of £44,000.'

'I averaged four lawns mowed every day and for each lawn mowed earned the Scout group £1.'

- Use active and descriptive words wherever you can. On page 14 is a list of words that may help you with your sentence constructions.
- When you are happy that you have covered absolutely every kind of task that you can think of that you have carried out in your working life (methodical working backwards through your life from your most recent job to your first should help), go through your list and indicate next to every statement which of the following categories it falls into: People, Information, Practical, Academic, Creative. For example:

Active and descriptive words

achieved
accomplished
approved
arranged for
assessed
assisted
authorized
budgeted
calculated
competed
compiled
completed
composed
conceived
consulted
controlled
cooperated
created
dealt with
delivered
demonstrated
designed

developed
devised
employed
established
estimated
expanded
facilitated
finalized
foresaw
forestalled
guided
identified
implemented
incorporated
initiated
instructed
learned
managed
motivated
negotiated
organized
participated

performed
planned
prepared
prioritized
produced
promoted
reorganized
researched
responded to
scheduled
set up
solved
strengthened
supervised
took responsi-
  bility for
trained
utilized
won
wrote

Maintained detailed budgets and reported to senior management at fortnightly intervals.   [Information]

Directed a team of eight, planning workloads and schedules, utilizing skills to the best advantage.
[People]

Ran a string of 15 freelance designers and illustrators.   [People]

Designed and made a tool box from scratch, making use of a limited range of available materials.
[Practical]

Studied computer design packages x, y and z on a one-year evening class at the East Langley College, passed end of year examinations with a merit.
[Academic]

Compiled a 24-page (1/2A4) guide to using office equipment for all new staff.   [Creative]

Produced a series of watercolours for use as Christmas cards, printed and sold in aid of the local church roof appeal.   [Creative]

Area 2: Education
- Write down in date order where you went to school and college, and give the dates.

- Write down the subjects in which you took public examinations, and the grades you achieved, along with the dates. Include not only narrow educational qualifications such as GCSEs or degrees, but any others you can think of: grade qualifications in the study of a musical instrument, for example, or recognized national qualifications in dance, drama, gymnastics and other sports.
- Write down any subjects that you disliked studying or subjects you failed in.
- Write down important positions you held while at school or college: e.g. head pupil, prefect, team captaincies, posts in the student union, on college administrative bodies.
- Write down prizes, scholarships or other measures of excellence achieved.
- Write down membership of teams, clubs and societies at school or college. Include a short description (not necessarily in full sentences) of everything you did as a member.
- Write down any activities you took part in outside school or college: community activities, membership of charitable bodies, looking after siblings, anything at all that you can think of.
- Write down any educational courses you have taken since leaving full-time education: training courses, refresher courses, even evening courses in cookery or languages, creative writing or advanced driving. Any form of education at all that has taken place since you left school or college.

- When you are sure that you have included all your educational experiences, run back over your notes and try to classify each entry into one of the categories you have been using for work experience: People, Information, Practical, Academic, Creative.

Area 3: Other skills and experience
- Here you should list every other kind of experience you have had, and, again, in full sentences if possible, break these often difficult-to-describe times in your life down into single tasks that you carried out. Don't miss anything out. If you have been bringing up a family, you probably have excellent time-management and organizational skills, which you need to be able to define and quantify. You will probably have liaised with other parents over child-minding arrangements or a rota for the school-run. If you have run a household (paying bills, organizing repairs, liaising with the landlord), you have important administrative skills. You will probably also have driving skills, cooking skills, painting and decorating skills, dressmaking and alterations skills. If you have cared for a sick or disabled relative or friend, identify the tasks that this involved. You probably have nursing and support skills and experience. Write it *all* down.
- Include membership of professional organizations, interest groups and pressure groups. Have you had articles published in the parish magazine, have you organized a bring and buy sale, have you raised money or been active at meetings? Keep your notes as specific as

you can, using full, concise sentences.
- Again, when you are satisfied that you have got everything, run through your sentences and categorize the tasks and activities under the same headings as before: People, Information, Practical, Academic, Creative.

When you have completed the tasks for Areas 1, 2 and 3, take a break. Go away and do something else for a while. If you can, during your break keep a pen and paper with you. Now that your brain has started working on remembering what tasks you have undertaken in your life, it will continue to work on it even while you are sleeping. Be ready to jot down new ideas as they pop into your head, and they will!

Analysing your skills

Next time you come back to your self-assessment (and you should not leave it too long – 24 hours is a maximum), read through the notes you have made on your three large pieces of paper and add anything that came to you during the break or comes to you as you read.

- Now take a new piece of paper and write at the top the following headings: People, Information, Practical, Academic, Creative.
- Go back to your task sentences and copy each one into the relevant column, improving them if you can, to make them as descriptive and concise as possible. In carrying out this part of the exercise you are categorizing your

skills and experiences, building up a picture of where your strengths and weaknesses are, and finding out really how rich and varied your life's experience has been.

- Now re-read every sentence you have written. If you had to mention one point of which you are most proud from each field, which one would it be? Mark it with the figure 1. If you could mention another, which one would it be? Mark this one with the figure 2. Go on doing this until you have pinpointed your top 10 experiences, skills or achievements. Then write down your greatest success, and next to it, put down your greatest failure.

By the time this part of the exercise is completed, you should be beginning to realize that the skills you have acquired, whatever they are, can be taken out of the context in which you developed or originally used them, and transferred into a new context: a job or new business venture, perhaps. These skills will now be referred to as 'transferable skills' for this reason.

What kind of person are you?

By now you probably have a pretty good idea of your skills profile: you should know what your specialist knowledge consists of and what categories your skills fall into. You should also have a clear idea of the chronology of your education and work experience. And above all, you should have a good strong list of your top 10 most important skills or experiences. Now you need to add to it a clear picture of your emotional and most private self: a study of your own temperament. Take a clean piece of paper and answer, using full sentences, as many as possible of the following questions:

- Do you like to work as a member of a team or as a team leader?
- Do you prefer a large company with a rigid hierarchical structure or a small, more informal company?
- Do you lose your temper quickly or are you a patient and even-tempered person?
- Do you keep up with current events?
- Do you like to work on long-term projects with no end in sight, or do you prefer to undertake a task that has a foreseeable completion point?
- Do you like to live in the middle of a big city? Or would you prefer a quiet suburb or the depths of the countryside?
- Do you prefer to have people around you most of the time, or do you like to be alone?
- Are you always late, or more often than not on time?
- Do you enjoy travelling or taking long journeys?
- Would you say that you are a physically active person, or are most of your pursuits sedentary?
- Do you enjoy meeting new people?
- Are you a religious person?
- Do you have strong commitments to political or charitable causes?
- Is it important to you to do well in the eyes of others, or are you content to do as well as you know how?
- Are you talkative?
- Do you dream about adventure in foreign places, or about

a cosy chair by the fire?

- Do you often do things on impulse? Do you regret them later? Or do you always weigh the pros and cons before doing anything?
- Do you like being in a crowd of people?
- Do you enjoy solving problems?
- Do you like to work unsupervised, or would you prefer to have someone defining your workload for you?
- Is money important to you? Do you feel unhappy when you can't buy the things you want?
- Would you say that you are independent and self-reliant, or do you like to have someone to share your concerns?
- Are you fashion-conscious: do you keep up with the latest trends?
- Are your hobbies more enjoyable or more important to you than your work?
- Do you enjoy working with words, with figures, with people, with objects?
- Would you feel unhappy if you were forced to move away from your home town permanently?
- Is your idea of status and personal identity linked to career success? Do you need an important job to feel good about yourself?
- Do you obey the rules, or do you like to bend them whenever it suits you?
- Do you have a large number of friends and acquaintances or just a handful of trusted friends?
- Is family life important to you?
- Do you have a handicap (of any type: physical, psycho-

logical, cultural) that stops you doing the things you want to do?
- Do you prefer to work indoors or in the open air?
- Do you respect authority?
- Do you enjoy teaching people to do things?
- Do you like to see fast results, or do you take pleasure in seeing something grow over a period of time.
- Do you enjoy studying or learning to do things?
- Are you a persuasive speaker?
- Are you plagued by ill-health?
- Do you worry a lot about security (housing, money, the future)? Or do you live from day to day with little thought for the future?
- Do you like to work with your hands or with your brain?
- Do you gain greatest satisfaction out of making things?

These questions are not designed as a sure-fire method of pinning down your personality. They should simply start you thinking about the kinds of situations you like or dislike, and about the kind of person you are in general. There are probably many other questions you could ask yourself along these lines. Don't worry if your answers are contradictory. We are all a mass of contradictions: that's what makes each one of us so interesting as people. And try not to pre-judge your answers. No-one but you will see your notes unless you want them to, so confess to yourself what you see as your failings, and boast to yourself about your strengths. But most important of all – don't lie to yourself about who and what you are.

The whole package

The sum of all this hard work should be a very wide-ranging description of you as an individual with skills, specialist knowledge, experience, academic prowess, and with a multi-faceted personality. This is the commodity you have to exchange in the market place.

Now you must decide the kinds of things you would like to receive in return.

Define your needs

In the new world of contract work, telecommuting, intermittent working and multiple job-holding, there is no reason to suffer working environments that don't suit us, long journeys to work each day, or roles that are overstressful, unless these come low on our list of priorities. In the past the main priority of most people has been to find a secure job and to stay in that job, rising through the pay-scale, as long as possible. In the past it has been enough for most people that they have a job, particularly in recent years, when these have become thin on the ground.

Employees have suffered being sent away from home for long periods, or have relocated with their company when they did not necessarily wish to do so, because a greater priority was to hold onto their jobs and the security they brought. In the future, companies will not be able to offer such security. Continuity of work will not be so important for its own sake, and the worker who moves from one employer to another will not be considered so much of a pariah, especially if he or she is undertaking contract work instead of 'permanent' employment.

But where does that leave us? Suddenly we find ourselves needing to make decisions about what we want out of life in the absence of job security and simple career progression. We should start to think about working environment, the journey to work, the kind of people we would like to work with (if at all), the rewards we most value, the dreams we have for the future. To make the following exercise work, be prepared to fantasize, note down ideals. Dream a little, dream a lot – your dreams may not be so impossible to realize once you start to analyse what exactly it would take to make them come true. Take another large sheet of paper and jot down your answers to the following:

- A doctor tells you that you have one year to live. How would you change your life for that last 12 months on earth?
- You win the lottery. What would you do, not only with the money, but also with the time the money buys for you – what would you do if you didn't have to work?
- If you had the opportunity to make enough money to survive doing something you enjoyed, what would that something be?
- If you could remove all the things you hate about your present or past working life, what would they be? Number them in order of priority.
- If you had the opportunity to make enough money to survive while working for a charitable or political cause, what would that cause be? And what skills would you be able to offer your cause?

- What do you see yourself doing in five years time? Where are you geographically, physically? Who is around you? What are you doing? Are you content?
- Visualize in the same way your life 10 years on, 20 years on.
- At the end of your life you must write a letter for posterity, telling your family and friends your fondest memories. What would you like those memories to have been?

Are you starting to build a picture of the kind of life you want to lead? And is your brain starting to tick away, wondering how to achieve it? How is your new job going to fit into your pattern? What will your new job bring that makes these dreams possible. Make a list of the things you will be looking for from an employer, client or customer – what will you be looking to receive in this exchange:

- Do you need a certain level of income?
- Do you want to work in a certain geographical location?
- Are hours of work important? Do you want to be flexible in your working hours?
- What type of work do you want to do?
- What kind of people do you want to work with?
- What kind of prospects are you looking for? Are you blindingly ambitious or would you be satisfied to continue doing the same job for the next 10 or 20 years?
- How much longer do you want to carry on working before you retire, start a family, leave the country to travel, start your own business?

- Is money the most important product of working, or are you more interested in achieving a high quality of life with time to spend on other pleasures? Or perhaps the satisfaction of working for a cause is more important than either of these.

It might be a good idea to keep the notes you have made. One day in the future you may undertake the same process again, and it will be interesting to see how your personal profile has changed in the intervening months or years. You could keep them in the same place as all your other work-related papers: national insurance and tax records, examination certificates, articles about you in the press, photographs of your work, etc., so that you have a complete dossier on yourself to remind you of how far you have come along your career path.

By now you have probably spent hours and possibly days thinking about yourself, you should have a pretty clear idea of the deal you are looking for in the work market: what you have to offer, and what you are looking for in return. After all that thinking it is probably a relief to know that now it is time to start doing something practical about finding work.

PLANNING THE SEARCH

'It's a recession when your neighbour loses his job: it's a depression when you lose yours.'

Harry S. Truman (1884–1972)

How many times have you heard people say so-and-so is lucky, he'll find a job in no time: Andrew down the road was lucky enough to find a new job within a month of being made redundant; Sarah decided to go back to work after the children went to school and a job just came along – how lucky she was? People who think this way believe that they need do very little, that things will simply happen to them, jobs will fall into their laps, that if they are lucky they will find work, and if not, well there is nothing they can do.

If luck is what it takes to find work, then there is a very easy way of increasing your quota of luck: put in as many hours a week as you can looking for work. The more time spent looking for work, the more chances you have of finding it. A person who spends 40 hours a week on their search has 40 times more chance of finding work than the person who spends one hour a week. Now there's luck for you.

At the same time, some people believe that there are people out there whose job it is to find work for them. While this is true, the person *most* interested in your search for work is yourself. Your partner or spouse may support you, your friends may be interested in how you are getting on, and staff at the careers service or Jobcentre are paid to help you find opportunities. But it matters to no-one more than you that you are successful in this endeavour, and so no-one can be expected to put as much effort into your search as you. In preparing to look for work, the fact to lodge in your mind, therefore, is that you have only yourself to rely on for the energy, motivation and organization it takes to succeed.

Be prepared to treat your search for work as a job in itself. Freelancers and self-employed people already do this: the tasks that make up their 'job' include looking for new clients and customers and landing new contracts. Indeed, the most successful self-employed people are those who have recognized that the search for work is an important part of their business and devote a fair amount of attention to it. As a business grows, it eventually requires a person who can devote herself to this task alone: a sales person. Very soon the lone sales person becomes an entire team, all of its members looking for clients and customers wherever they can, constantly seeking the people who need their company's products or service. In a world where permanent jobs are becoming more and more scarce, the successful job-hunters will be the ones who treat job-hunting as a job.

Work-search HQ

To carry out the work-search effectively, it is important to have a settled place from which to do it: a work-search headquarters. The space you choose should be private and quiet. In terms of furniture you will need a desk or table, a chair and, ideally, a typing machine (a typewriter or word-processor). A telephone with an answerphone would also be extremely useful, and shelf space or a filing cabinet is handy for filing copies of correspondence and the information on companies and prospective employers you are going to be gathering.

If you cannot devote a whole room to your work-search activities, look for a section of a room you could set aside. The important point is that you should be able to leave your bits and pieces there and not have them disturbed by anyone until you want to go back to them. If you really have to use the kitchen table, find a large and sturdy box in which you can store your papers, files and equipment while the table is in use for other things.

Make sure that other people understand that while you are in your 'office' you should not be disturbed, and that objects should not be taken from your desk or box without your permission. There is nothing more frustrating than having a prospective employer call to arrange an interview and not being able to find a pen that works. If your last decent envelope is used to send a letter to Aunt Mavis, you may miss the post with an urgent application, and that could cost you the work you have been striving for. If you come back to your typewriter to find that someone has worn out the ribbon (it's six o'clock and the shops are shut), but you must get the application there tomorrow morning, you're beaten before you've even started. Your search for work is a serious activity – as serious as doing the work itself – and your family or housemates must understand that your typewriter is not a toy, and that your papers are valuable to you.

Your office should be quiet if at all possible. Obviously, it is very difficult to concentrate while your partner is gossiping with a friend or the children are watching cartoons on television. If you are already having problems motivating yourself, it is very easy to allow a distraction (such as a favourite television programme, or a visit from a friend) to disrupt your entire day's work. Equally, what kind of impression would a prospective employer get if she were to call up to hear that racket going on in the background and you getting the information wrong because you can't hear properly?

If it is impossible to avoid sharing your space with others, perhaps establishing a working day with them would help. Agree to be out and about at certain times of the day, in exchange for time at home during which you can expect to be left in peace.

Equipment

At the start of your search, ensure you have the necessary stationery and office equipment to enable you to administer your 'business' in a professional manner. You will need some, if not all, of the following items:

- Plain white or off-white A4 (210 x 297 mm) writing paper to be used to type or print CVs, letters and other written communications. A4 is the standard size used in offices, and most files are made to take this size. Smaller paper may get lost in the heap and larger paper will be a nuisance to the recipient. Avoid coloured paper unless you are sure that when it is photocopied (perhaps for distribution among the directors of a target company) your letter or CV is still perfectly legible. This kind of paper is categorized by weight. The heavier the paper, the better quality it is. Paper that is 70 g/m^2 or above should be good enough. If you have the money, invest in paper with a watermark, or laid paper (heavy paper which has a series of parallel lines embedded into it).

- Envelopes that match your writing paper in colour, weight and size. A stationer should be able to advise you on which to use. The envelopes most used in offices are classified C5: A4 paper is folded into thirds to make it fit into these envelopes.
- A pen. Choose the pen that makes your handwriting look best. If possible, buy a good-quality pen and make sure that no-one else uses it. A couple of biros are useful to make jottings and notes, but avoid using them for applications. Black ink is always recommended for filling out application forms and writing covering letters. Some say this is because it gives the impression that the writer is forthright and not wishy-washy. But really the point is, once again, that your letter or application is likely to be photocopied or faxed, and black ink shows up better than blue ink on the copy. Avoid any other colours of ink, which are too whimsical to give a professional impression.
- Stapler and staples.
- Hole punch.
- A stock of first-class stamps. Second-class stamps may be cheaper but they will be a false economy when mailing

job applications: you will need to be first in line for an interview (see page 56–8), so time is of the essence. Also, a second-class stamp implies that you do not consider your application an urgent matter, an impression to be avoided.

- An A4 lever-arch file and dividers. You will be using these to file copies of your communications to prospective employers, and their responses to you, along with copies of job advertisements, newspaper and magazine articles and any other information you have collected during your research.
- An A4 desk diary or large notebook that you can turn into a diary (see page 58–61).
- A pocket-sized notebook for jotting down information you come across in conversation with other people. You will need to be ready to pick up on any information that comes your way – any time.
- An address book, or a card file or computer database system for storing information about people you meet or hear of, people who may help you or who have helped you in your search for work (see page 59–62).
- A supply of blank postcards for use as quick thank-you notes. If you have the money, have your name, address and telephone number printed across the top of the writing side of the postcards, otherwise add these in handwriting when you use the card.
- Supplies for your typewriter or word-processor and printer: toner cartridges, ribbons, diskettes, etc. You may also want to buy poorer quality paper to use for typed

notes or copies of letters you have sent out.

- Cards or stickers with your name, address and contact numbers on them. These will come in very handy if you are serious about making as many contacts as you can. What good is a contact made if he can't remember your name and lost the paper napkin on which he wrote your phone number?

Getting into a routine

At the start of your search, decide how long you are going to devote to looking for work. You may decide that you will give yourself three months in which to find something that really fits the bill: work that is exciting and stimulating, using all your skills to the full. Sadly, however, it may not be possible to find such a position, and so after a space of time, you must consider taking stop-gap work while still looking for something more suitable.

The length of the period you choose will depend to a certain extent on your assets and your responsibilities. Ask yourself how long can your family survive without you earning money to help support them? How long will it be before your assets have dwindled to nothing and all you have is the social security payments to live on? Make a survey of your financial assets and try to assess your outgoings week by week to come to a deadline by which you should have found work.

Don't forget that most employers ask you to work a period of time 'in hand'. If you are being paid a monthly salary, expect to wait a month until you get paid. This can be extremely painful, particularly if a long period of employment has left your savings depleted. While having to pay out for travel, lunch and work clothes, you are still not being paid yourself. (However, if you find yourself in this situation, ask for advice at the Jobcentre or benefit office, as you may be entitled to temporary financial help.)

Now start to plan your day-to-day activities. Set yourself a regular start time (say, 9:30 a.m.) and a regular finish (say 5:30pm), and give yourself a set time for lunch (say, 1 p.m.– 2 p.m.). Make sure that by 9:30 a.m. you are dressed and ready to work, just as if you were turning up for a job as someone else's employee. Be disciplined about your timekeeping and try to establish a routine. This will ensure that you put in the requisite amount of work, but it also has another and more important effect.

If you have been used to going to work regularly at a certain time each day, you will greatly miss the habit of doing so if you suddenly find yourself cut adrift. Making a habit out of routine is the easiest way to make yourself stay active. People without routines or the work habit drift around aimlessly and run the risk of falling into depression (see page 43–7), whereas people with a routine have things to do, and will soon have places to go and people to meet. They have a reason to get out of bed in the morning, and, if they have achieved the targets they set themselves (see page 35–6), they have a reason to feel good about a day's work well done.

Don't let your appearance go. Always dress as smartly as you can, and keep yourself well-groomed. The reason for this is twofold. The first is that keeping your appearance up to scratch tends to keep you in good spirits. The second is that you never know when you might meet a prospective employer. Imagine that the owner of the corner shop is looking for a shop assistant. Will she want to employ you if she knows you as the person who comes in at midday looking like he has just fallen out of bed, unshaven, tousled hair, a dirty T-shirt and ragged sweater? Be prepared for opportunities to present themselves at the most unexpected moments.

Time-management

Most office workers are familiar with the principles of time-management. In brief, they are:

- List and prioritize your tasks, numbering them in order of importance. If your tasks need to be done by a certain time or date, add this information to your list. Prioritize urgent tasks over less urgent tasks, even if the less pressing jobs are the ones you prefer to do.
- Assess the amount of time it will take you to complete a task and set aside enough time to do it.
- Do it when it is supposed to be done: don't put it off.
- Set achievable targets for a days' work: don't make a list 100 items long when it is clear that you cannot finish them all in the time you have given yourself. It is very dispiriting not to be able to see the end of a task or process. Be reasonable, but don't be too easy on yourself.
- Be able to quantify your achievements day by day (so many letters sent, that difficult phone call made, this information found, the contact book updated), and reward yourself by giving yourself time off, or buying yourself a small gift or having a night out.

Use your diary to plan your days. There will be some tasks you will be doing every day, such as reading and answering your post, and there will be some tasks that you do only on certain days (checking new vacancies at the Jobcentre will probably be done twice a week, and picking up a copy of the local newspaper to check situations vacant will probably happen only once a week). Some tasks happen only once every so often, and cannot be predicted (a lunchtime drink with a contact or friend, a job interview, an assessment at a recruitment consultancy). However regularly or routinely you plan to carry out your tasks, write them down in your diary. As you do so, you will be assessing whether you will have time to accomplish everything you have set yourself to do in a day. If it seems you will not have enough time to do all the things on your list, mark out the most important and pressing tasks and do them first. Postpone less important tasks to the next day, but beware of doing so indefinitely. Make a conscious decision to reschedule, and if you have to in order for you to remember, put a mark next to them so that you know that you should not reschedule them again.

Each day, tick off the tasks that you have accomplished. At the end of the day look through the list. It really can be quite impressive, and very satisfying to know that you have done all you set out to do. In that knowledge you can allow yourself a relaxing evening at home or a night out with friends.

Most ready-made diaries are too small to be useful workbooks. An alternative is to buy an A4 ruled notebook. Devote one 'spread' (of two facing pages) to a day. Plot out the hours of the day on the right-hand page and write in your appointments as they are arranged. On the left-hand page list the tasks you have set yourself to do and leave space for notes. There is an example on pages 38–9.

Planning for leisure

When planning your 'working' week, make sure that you make time for leisure activities. All work and no play makes everyone dull people, even if they are not being paid for their work. Winding down after a good day's labour is a very important part of staying healthy. Leisure activities reduce stress and can take your mind off worries that lead to anxiety.

Keeping records

It is important to keep records of all contacts made during your search for work. Everyone you speak to should be entered into your address book, card file or computer database. The latter two methods are useful because the formats allow you to make notes on the people concerned (how you met them, when you met and what you discussed), and to cross-refer them to other contacts. Of course, none of these methods of keeping information works unless you are prepared to keep them up to date, and you should try to make time to do so every week. You might like to use the format on page 41.

Correspondence and research file

Keep copies of any letters you write and any applications you fill in. Carbon copies from a typewriter are good enough, but you will need to photocopy application forms. Also keep letters

Monday 16th January 1997

TASKS

✓ *Deal with post*

✓ *Buy Morning Courier and check computing sits vac*

✓ *Applications arising from MC sits vac*

Call John Brewer (friend of Carol, works at Crescent Court Communications) to arrange a drink.

Call Carol and thank her for the contact

Write thank-you note to Judy Moore at Parkside for help last Friday

NOTES

White & Dover interview: Friday 20th Jan?

Monday 16th January 1997

9:00	*Office*
10:00	
11:00	
12:00	
1:00	
2:00	*Call Mr Jenkins (White & Dover Ltd) to arrange meeting*
3:00	*Library: research Tanner & Sons*
4:00	
5:00	
Evening	*Drink: Adrian Jones (ex Tanner & Sons), Bull and Arrow 6:30*

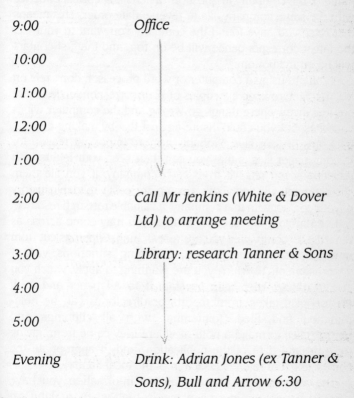

from anyone you come into contact with in your search for work. File all this correspondence in alphabetical order by the name of the company in question. When filing correspondence with the same company, file in reverse date order. This means that once you have found the company you want in your file, the latest correspondence will be on top, and the first contact will be on the bottom.

If you are using a computer or word processor, don't rely on the machine to keep file copies of your correspondence. There are instances where things go wrong and the computer wipes your files, but you could insure against this by making diskette back-ups of your files. Probably a more important reason for making paper files is that you can then keep your letters with the letters you receive from each company. If you file them correctly, you will soon have a complete, easily readable history of your contact with that company: a valuable research resource.

Keep in your file also any articles you may come across as regards the companies you are researching. Clippings cut from newspapers and magazines (including situations vacant advertisements to which you are planning to apply, which you should *always* keep) can be stapled to A4 paper and filed. Photocopies taken from reports or directories can be hole-punched and filed. Remember with all clippings and photocopies to make a note of where they came from, giving the title and date of the publication, and, if appropriate the source (e.g. the reference section of the local library).

The advantage of keeping all the information you have gathered together in one place is that when making an application or writing a letter, or refreshing your memory

(front)

Name: Judy Moore
Company: Parkside Ltd
Address: 51 Market Mall, Sackston SN1 6UP
Telephone: 01234 7654321
Position: Information Officer
Cross-references:
Jack Parks (Managing Director)

(reverse)

NOTES:
12/1/97 JM sent company report and
answered questions on phone
16/1/95 Thank-you note sent

before an interview or meeting, you have it all there in one place to browse through at your leisure. Failing to keep track of your research in this way will, unless you have a photographic memory, destroy all your efforts to gather information and build up a picture of the people and companies in your field (see pages 50–3).

Even if you have been interviewed by a company and did not succeed in getting the job on offer, you may find that the company calls you 10 months later to offer you a similar position. With a reference file on your shelf you can go back and find out what job was on offer the first time round and at what salary, who interviewed you, and even what you felt after the interview. When your second interview comes around, you will be in fantastic position to impress the interviewer with your professionalism. And if you have been keeping an eye on the press in the meantime and have kept clippings about the firm, you should have enough information stored away to appear interested, clued-in and, most importantly, employable.

At the same time, anyone who shows that he or she is capable of organizing information is instantly a more attractive proposition to an employer than someone who cannot. While you are searching for work using this method, you are learning and practising time-management, research and administration skills that could stand you in good stead, particularly if you are looking into supervisory, managerial or administrative positions. So when asked at the interview, what have you been doing with your time while you have been without paid work, you can describe your research techniques and information storage and retrieval systems, and your new administrative skills, just for a start. Furthermore, you are also learning how to motivate and discipline yourself without the proximity of a boss. This is an excellent way to find out whether you would be suited to working at home or to go into business for yourself. *Collins Pocket Reference Office Organizer* has more information on filing, keeping a diary, and other administrative skills.

Keep your chin up

Most of us rely on our jobs to provide us with a large part of our life. Our workplace probably provides us with friends and acquaintances, and many leisure activities can stem from contacts made at work. At the same time, the way our job is going (promotions, pay rises, the key to the executive washroom) gives us a measure of our success as people. As already discussed in this chapter, a permanent job also provides us with routine, a set pattern for our daily tasks. When we find ourselves without paid work, we feel suddenly adrift with seemingly no motivation. This change from being busy with work to being without work therefore has ramifications in many parts of our lives. No wonder we can so easily feel angry, confused, hurt and, eventually, depressed when all this is taken away from us. The rug has been pulled out from under our feet and we may well topple over as a result.

Experts say that the greatest hazards of being without paid work, particularly for a long period of time, are depression and loneliness, and that the longer you are out of work, the more likely you are to become vulnerable to them. Here are some notes to help avoid depression and ways to keep morale up when things seem hopeless:

- If you have been made redundant, remember that it is functions and not people that are made redundant. Just because one company decides to pull out of your field, it doesn't mean to say that they are all going to do the same. And even if they are, your skills are transferable to other functions in other fields. You are perfectly adaptable.
- As discussed earlier (page 33–7) structure your days and keep to a routine. If you have formed work habits and maintained them while you are without work, you are less likely to succumb to apathy and depression when the going gets tough. Trying to maintain your routine between jobs helps you resist the shock of losing the routine of work when you lose your job and then having to relearn it when you find a new one.
- Plan your tasks and reward yourself when you have completed them satisfactorily. Pride yourself on doing everything you set yourself to the best of your ability. Don't allow yourself to believe that things don't matter so much just because you are not being paid for doing them.
- Keep an eye on your physical health and well-being. Many people who are not working are entitled to reduced prices at gyms and sports centres. If you don't already do regular exercise, start, but don't be too tough on yourself. If you can, combine your fitness activities with something social: the chatter of an aerobics class is better than the solitude of the gym. If you normally drive everywhere, look into buying a pushbike. This will not only save you money on petrol and help reduce air pollution, partic-

ularly in our car-packed cities, but it will also make you fitter. Older people who are not used to exercise or those with ongoing health problems should consult a doctor before embarking on a new exercise regime.

- Make sure that you eat properly. While being without work may mean that you are short of money, the one thing you should never skimp on is meals. Eat a regular, well-balanced diet and try to keep down levels of smoking and drinking. Irregular meals and reduced intake of essential vitamins and minerals can lead to a feeling of stress and anxiety.

- Socialize with people as much as you can: loneliness is a dangerous depressive. Choose a mixture of people who are in work and who are out of work so that you have a balanced view of life on both sides of the fence. However, stay away from negative people: those who are always complaining – the lame ducks of this world. Go for contented people who have a sunny outlook. They will help to keep you buoyant.

- Find a mentor, someone who will agree to act as cheerleader and commiserator. Someone you see once a week and to whom you can pour out all your frustrations and with whom you can celebrate your successes. Someone who can talk common sense to you when you can't see the wood for the trees. This person could be your partner, although you may find you rely on that person's emotional support a little too often, exhausting him or her in the process. It is better to find someone who is a little more detached, and who can go away to recharge their own batteries before they see you again.

- Find unpaid work to do while you have the time. You may want to set yourself the task of painting the house, building a garden shed, or doing something else similarly constructive, or it may be that you want to become a helper at a local boys' club, or volunteer for charity work. Don't allow this work to get in the way of your search for paid work, but think about how you can exhibit it to prospective employers as yet another string to your bow. Who knows, you may discover a talent or vocation that leads you down a work path completely different to the one you are contemplating. A former sales rep could become a carpenter; a former insurance broker could discover a talent for making musical instruments; a former foundry worker could discover that he can make money as a market gardener.

- Always have other opportunities lined up if you can. If you get a job interview, don't cancel others, and don't stop looking. Don't stop looking even if you are offered a permanent position. Only stop looking when you have finalized all the negotiations and can count yourself in work again. The reason for this is that having other irons in the fire can make the difference psychologically if you are rejected at the interview you were pinning your hopes on. Knowing that there is another opportunity waiting just down the line will help to cushion the blow.

- As someone who is not in paid work, the one luxury you can count on is time. Use the time you have to do all those things you want to do when you are working but don't have the time. Visit exhibitions, go for walks in the country, visit your relatives, go to stately homes and gardens. Make the most of your time. Once you have found work again, you never know when you will get another chance.

- Set yourself a time limit. If you have not found work in that time, change your strategy. Find a part-time job, or a temporary job, but don't stop looking for your ideal.

Now that your work-search office is in place and you have planned your day-to-day routine to allow for hard footwork but also some leisure, the time has come to discover where to go and who to talk to to find your way to work.

AVENUES TO WORK

'A man must make his opportunity, as oft as find it.'
Francis Bacon (1561–1626)

Where you go from here depends very much on your starting point. If you are just about to leave school, you may still be trying to compile a shortlist of jobs you may like to do. If you are a seasoned worker with 10 or 20 years behind you, you will have a much better idea of the kinds of opportunities there are out there, which ones you are best qualified to take advantage of and which ones fit the bill as far as your lifestyle plans are concerned. However, if you are planning to change careers completely, you may still need to do some initial research on jobs and professions, to get a clear idea of which direction you should be taking.

Once you have defined your goal, it will be time to start searching, using every possible avenue, leaving no stone unturned, until you find either a permanent full-time job with an employer, part-time work or temporary work with one or more companies, or start to build a list of clients interested in making use of your services on a contract or freelance basis. You may even be planning to start your own small business; but whatever your aim, the following advice should be pertinent.

What job do I want to do?

Having carried out the exercises in chapter 1 (pages 7–26), you know what kinds of things you are good at, and you have taken stock of your educational qualifications. You have a list of transferable skills and realise that they can be taken with you from one job to another. You also know, in theory anyway, what kind of working life you want to pursue. So how do you find out what job you should be looking for?

A start is to make use of the information available at your local library. The library services sees the provision of careers and business information as one of its main priorities, and so most of them carry (usually in the reference section) a range of brochures, directories and books giving a wealth of information on jobs, careers and professions and what they entail. Probably the most useful of these in this context is the COIC's *Occupations* directory, an annual which lists many types of work and gives detailed information on what the work entails, prospects, pay and conditions, entry requirements and training. Browsing in the library will also bring to light books that treat work in various specialized areas, with titles such as *Working with Animals*, *Jobs with Computers*, *Working in Engineering*.

Alternatively, you may be planning to achieve certain qualifications, and want to know what opportunities you would have if you did so. There are a number of publications that would give you advice from this angle as well.

In any visit to the local library, the most important person is the librarian. He or she is a fount of knowledge on a wide range of subjects, and can, more often than not, point you in the right direction or answer general questions. He or she can also save you time by suggesting publications you might read and showing you where they are in the library.

Incidentally, while at the library, keep your eye out for interesting information pinned to notice boards. As the centre of your community, a great deal of information about what's going on, and particularly requests for voluntary workers, appears on library notice boards. Treat them as a resource like any other and make a point of checking them regularly.

If you are a school pupil, student or recent graduate, you will probably be able to make use of the library at your institution's careers centre. Again, take advantage of the specialist knowledge of the careers advisor or librarian, who should be able to give you invaluable information (free of charge) on many different career paths.

At the start of your worksearch, find out about the possibilities for training and retraining. Your Jobcentre or librarian should be able to give you some suggestions and find further information for you. You may also be eligible for government work-experience schemes and executive jobsearch seminars. If you are planning to go out on your own, you may be eligible for a grant. Check this with your Jobcentre as soon as you can.

Talk to people

When you have some idea of the kind of thing you would like to pursue, try to find people who are already doing the job, or have done the job in the past, and talk to them about it. Get as clear a picture as you can about what the work entails: the hours; pay and working conditions; the tasks involved; qualifications needed to start; on-going training; the prospects for promotion; how often people move from one employer to the next; whether there are shortages of labour in the field; whether jobs in the field are disappearing; who the major employers are.

When you know which employers are active in your field, find someone who can set up a meeting with the person who hires workers in your field. If you cannot find a personal link with this person, write and ask for a meeting. At this stage all you want is to discuss the work in the abstract: what qualifi-cations would you need to have to stand a chance of getting a job? what are the usual methods of entry into the business? where does the employer usually advertise? how many staff does the employer need to do the job? are any changes taking place that might cause the employer to hire more people in this role or fewer?

Do not ask for a job: the conversation can include advice on your case specifically, but asking outright for a job at this stage will probably only alienate a good contact. People love to be able to give advice, but they may not have a job to offer you and they hate that awkward feeling when they are put in the position of having to say no.

If you have a meeting like this arranged, prepare for it as you would for an interview. Take a copy of your CV and hand it over when you leave (make sure it gives your telephone number). If you have made a good impression, your details will be filed with other personnel information, and if suitable work comes up, you may get a phone call.

Structuring a conversation

Fact-finding conversations like the one mentioned above, whether they are with parents, other relatives, neighbours, friends or friends of friends, are your first steps in the process of networking, a process that will be very important to you in the search for work (see pages 58–61).

Some people feel awkward about asking people for their time to have a conversation: they fear becoming tongue-tied or having the conversation dry up or they fear suddenly finding themselves out of their depth, not understanding what the conversation is about, appearing stupid, foolish or 'green'. You are not alone with these fears – many people feel the same way. The remedy is to plan what you would like to discuss. Make notes on the questions you want to ask. Take a list with you and refer to it when you cannot think of what to say next. Don't worry about how other people think this looks. Far from seeming foolish, you will be showing that you want to make your conversation productive, and that you have cared enough about the meeting to prepare in advance. If you have done some effective homework beforehand (finding out about what a job entails in theory, for instance, by reading up on it at the library), you should never feel out of your depth. Furthermore, if you read your profession's trade magazine and keep an eye on the relevant specialist sections of the daily press, you should be clued-up enough to comment on current events in your industry.

When setting up a meeting, give your contact an idea of how long you need: 20 minutes is probably the most you are going to get. When you have set a time be punctual, and do not overstay your welcome. If you have asked for 20 minutes wind up the conversation at that time. That is unless your contact is in the process of outlining a job vacancy to you! Take your cue from your host.

Seeking out the work

There are many avenues to work, and some of them will be more likely to yield results than others. Here are some of the most common:

- responding to advertisements;
- personal contacts and recommendations (networking);
- recruitment agencies, employment agencies and headhunters;
- using jobcentres and careers services;
- professional registers and other lists;
- advertising your availability;
- speculative applications to companies not currently advertising.

In order to be successful in your search for work it is important to follow as many of these avenues as are appropriate for the type of work you are looking for, and to pursue them all at once. Keep working at them, going over the same or slightly different ground again and again until things start to move.

Advertised vacancies

Situations vacant advertisements appear in many places: the national daily press; the local press; noticeboards in supermarkets; in shop windows and at factory gates; on club bulletin boards; in trade magazines and specialist and professional journals; on Ceefax, on the Internet and on local radio. However, while this is the most visible part of the job market, a surprisingly small proportion of permanent positions are filled through advertising, particularly in national newspapers. The cost of advertising is often high and so employers often try other methods of finding recruits first. At the same time, the competition for advertised vacancies is stiff: if 500 people have applied for the same single job that you have, and we assume that most of these are, like you, suitably qualified, then you still have only a one in 500 chance of getting the job. However, you should not reject this avenue out of hand, but combine replying to advertisements with continuing to search by the other methods described later.

At the start of your search, make a list of all the places you might expect to find situations vacant advertisements that might relate to your search and decide how you are going to cover them on a regular basis.

The national press
Most daily newspapers regularly devote certain days to certain areas of work, and weekend newspapers usually have a selection of more general and usually high-level executive posts. Find out which newspapers cover your field and on which days. Write a note in your diary to collect copies of those papers as soon as they come out, and ensure that you allocate enough time on that day to respond to relevant advertisements (see page 38–9).

The local press
The majority of jobs advertised in the local press will be based in your area. If you want to make a move to a new geographical location, you may be able to have the paper local

to the region you are targeting sent to you by the publisher (a trip to the area or a call to a contact living there would bring you the information you need). Local newspapers can include a high proportion of part-time or temporary work, and usually include clerical, administrative and semi-skilled work. It is quite rare to find higher-level managerial or specialist work advertised in local newspapers.

Again, find out which days the papers are published and make sure that you get your copy early. If your newsagent does not deliver until late in the day, try going to the offices of the publisher to get a copy earlier.

Periodicals, trade magazines and journals

If you are in a specialist field, you probably already know which periodicals, magazines and journals are read by your colleagues and customers, and which have situations vacant sections. If you are just entering a field of work, a question to your librarian will help you find out which publications there are to choose from. Half an hour in a large newsagent should bring results, but remember that some publications are sent out by subscription only and therefore will never appear on newsagents' shelves. If you are still in work, keep an eye open for the titles of magazines read by your colleagues (what trade publication does your boss read?), and what specialist magazines appear in your company's reception area. Find out where your company and its competitors advertise for their staff.

If your work is linked to a professional organization, such as a trade union, society or association, that body may also publish regular journals. Call the body in question to find out about them. *Whitaker's Almanack* (in the library) gives a full list of contact details. *The Writers' and Artists' Yearbook* (A & C Black, published annually), while compiled for freelance writers, journalists, illustrators and photographers, gives a very full list of magazines and newspapers published in the UK, and an equally useful classified index.

If you can afford to, take out a subscription to your chosen publication. Paying by subscription can often turn out cheaper if you plan to take the publication regularly.

Reading specialist publications will keep you in touch with current vacancies, but will also keep you abreast of current events and issues in your industry. Being knowledgeable in your field can only help when making conversation with contacts, talking to interviewers or having smart ideas about who to target with speculative applications (see pages 66–71).

Move fast

In the case of all jobs advertised in these ways, be prepared to act instantly. Many advertisers, deluged with replies, may decide to open only the first few responses in the first instance. Make sure that yours is among them. A speedy response is only possible if you have planned your search and organized your information in advance. It's no use seeing an advertisement for your dream job only to spend a week getting your CV together. Even if advertisements give closing dates, get your application there by return of post to be sure of being considered. Anything else is a waste of time and money.

Hand deliver your application if at all possible, or send it by special delivery so that it arrives in the first post the following day. If you can afford it, and know the name of the person making the appointment (call up to find out if the name given on the advert is that of the person doing the hiring or of the personnel officer), send your application by motorcycle courier. If this is the job you have been dreaming about and you are sufficiently confident, send your application by Federal Express. A brightly-coloured FedEx envelope gives the impression of urgency and has a novelty factor that ensures that the addressee sits up and pays attention. The last two suggestions may sound a little over-the-top, but there are instances in which they have worked, getting the applicant past the first stage and into the interview room. One of them might work for you.

It is even more important to pick up the papers early if you are looking in the local press. This is because in these newspapers it is more likely that advertisers will give you a phone number to call, rather than an address to write to. Recruiting in this way can be very disruptive to the recruiter (if they resort to it they are probably desperate for someone), and so they will probably set a time limit after which they will not take any more calls. They will probably also have a target number of people to interview, and if they speak to this number of likely candidates within half an hour of the advertisement being published, the 'position filled' signs will go up and your chance will be gone. See pages 123–7 for more on the techniques of telephone interviewing.

If the job is advertised in a shop window or at the factory gate, go in at once to make enquiries. Keep an eye out all the time for places in which jobs might be advertised and make it one of your routine tasks to visit these places. Write the activity down in your diary to ensure that you don't miss any of them. When making the rounds in this way, dress as if you were going to an interview – you may be interviewed on the spot by a hard-pressed manager desperate for help. Do not rule yourself out by the way you look.

The principles of networking

Making friends and acquaintances and using them to help you become aware of opportunities (for that is what networking is), is probably your best bet when it comes to finding the work you want. Networking is simple, but it takes some legwork:

- Make use of all your existing contacts: relatives, friends, business acquaintances, current clients, chance acquaintances. Broaden your circle of friends and acquaintances by introducing yourself to new neighbours, work colleagues, people at your place of worship. Strike up an acquaintance with the people at your bank, your corner shop or post office. Remember things they say, and try to find reasons to start a conversation next time round if this seems appropriate.
- Make a list of all the people you know. Write down their addresses or phone numbers. Make notes on what they do for a living and where they work. Use your card file, address book or computer database to keep these records in order (see page 37). Don't be afraid to talk to people about themselves. Most of us prefer to talk about ourselves than about anything else, and so you can only elicit a good response by being interested in what others do and think.

- Tell all your contacts you are looking for work. Write to them, telephone them, seek them out at work or in the pub, at the swimming pool, on the football field, at the tennis club. If you are unemployed, there is no need to feel ashamed: everyone will be in the same boat sooner or later. There is no reason to keep your situation a secret and every reason to advertise your job search to as many people and by as many means as you can. (By the way, you could always add this information to the announcement on your answerphone, to make sure that all your callers get the message, even when you are out.) Let people know that you are in the market, and if your direct contacts cannot help you, ask them if they can put you in touch with someone who may be able to. The harder you work at this, the more people who know about your search, the greater the chances that, sooner or later, someone will say, 'I know a person you should talk to'. Don't be surprised if your contacts say they cannot help on a first approach. You may find that after a couple of days they come back with a bright idea that could be just the help you need. Remember not to ask your contacts directly for a job, but for advice and information. Having to say 'no' makes people feel awkward.
- When a contact does come up with a lead, ask her if you can use her name when you contact the person to whom you are being recommended. Then, when you call to ask for an appointment or to set up a meeting, use your contact as your introduction: 'I'm a friend of Jean Waters, who is a manager on the xyz project. She suggested I get

in touch with you...' If no particular job is on offer, simply discuss the work, and avoid the temptation to ask for a job outright.

- Always leave your phone number with new contacts, and check that old contacts still have your number. If you can afford to, have calling cards printed, giving your contact details. If you meet with someone in the industry who is likely to be hiring, give them a copy of your CV for their files.

- Stay in touch with your contacts. If a friend gives you the name of someone who can help, follow it up and then report back to him. Tell him how things went. Thank him for the contact (either with a note or with a phone call). Keep him informed as to what you are doing. In this way people will continue to remember you, and this may lead to the connection you have been waiting for.

- Do not expect things to happen without putting in any effort yourself. This is not a method of getting other people to do the work for you. Do not expect others to put themselves out if you are not prepared to follow up their leads and work hard to make a good impression with their contacts. Remember that whenever they refer you to a contact of theirs, your conduct is likely to reflect on their judgement. It is important to leave a good impression for their sakes as well as for your own.

- Remember: the wider the net the more likely you are to bring in the big fish you have been trawling for.

If you are still in work when you begin your search you will need to be a great deal more discreet than this, but there is no reason why you should not start to sound out contacts without dropping yourself in it. Ideally, of course, you should have discussed your wish to move with your senior in the hope that he will offer you more money, more flexible working hours, or recommend you to the head of the department that covers the new kind of work you want to do.

Using recruitment consultants

Recruitment consultants (rec cons, for short) are private companies that specialize in finding staff for their clients. The client companies (that is, the prospective employers) make a request for a worker with particular qualifications and abilities. The recruitment consultant puts together a shortlist of suitable candidates. These candidates will already have been screened by the recruitment consultant. You may have seen specific jobs advertised by recruitment consultants in newspapers and magazines. These may be real jobs that the recruitment consultant needs to fill, but may also be dummy jobs designed to attract potential candidates.

Many recruitment consultants specialize in certain fields: business, the media, banking, stockbroking, marketing, etc. They will most often place workers in the middle-management or low-level professional brackets (trainee managers, middle-level secretarial support staff, etc.). Keeping your eyes open when reading the situations vacant pages, or a glance at the Yellow Pages should produce the names and contact numbers of a shortlist of recruitment consultants specializing in your field, and you should contact them. If you can, however, it is always best to choose a recruitment consultant by recommendation, or at least one whose reputation you know to be good.

Send a short covering letter and enclose your CV. Your aim in doing this is to be invited for a meeting, which you should take as seriously as a job interview. The consultant will be vetting you as a first screen for a potential employer. He or she will also be concerned that you will give a good impression that reflects well on the consultancy when you go for interviews.

Recruitment consultants usually make their money by charging the employer a percentage of the employee's first year's salary. Ensure that this is the case and that you will not be charged if they find work for you. You should not be asked to pay a registration fee.

Because recruitment consultants are paid by their clients and not by you, don't expect them to spend time looking after you. While it is in their interest to ensure you have information about the prospective employer's business when attending an interview, they will rarely have time to give you career advice.

Equally, it is often the case that recruitment consultants only work with the latest batch of applicants they have. If you are not placed within, say, a month, your application will 'go stale'. As time goes on, the consultant remembers your details less and less clearly and is more and more unlikely to put you on the interview shortlist even if a suitable opening appears. To avoid this happening, keep in touch with your contact at the consultancy (without becoming a nuisance). Send a thank-you note when you have been to an interview, or call to explain what happened (it is always useful to discuss unsuccessful interviews – the consultant may well have been told why you were not selected and that information is valuable for the next time). Do all you can to keep your name and face in front of the consultant for as long as possible. If you have had no interviews for a month or so, register with other consultants.

Even if you are placed, stay in touch with the consultant. You never know when you may be looking for work again, or when she might contact you with the offer of an even better job.

Employment agencies

Employment agencies are similar to recruitment consultancies, but there are some differences. Many employment agencies cover temporary and part-time work, as well as full-time, permanent placements. They usually cover the building trade, clerical, administrative and secretarial work, accountancy, nursing and catering. A number of agencies have recently opened, however, that place computer operators in specialist fields such as design, multimedia and illustration.

Use the same methods as you would when approaching a recruitment consultant. Treat meetings as interviews and stay in touch. It is possible with employment agencies to simply walk in for a meeting without an appointment, and this is less time-consuming than writing a letter. Be prepared to fill in an application form for the agency's records and expect to be tested. Take your CV with you to remind you of details when filling in the application form. Also, take copies of your qualification certificates in case you are asked for them.

Many employment agencies will assess your skills and qualifications and might suggest training to improve your chances of employment.

Headhunters

Headhunters are networkers par excellence. They make their commission by matchmaking executives with a high profile or long record of excellence with companies (often multinationals) who have (unadvertised) openings. Headhunters do not take speculative applications. If you are to be placed through a headhunter, you will know about it when they contact you!

Using Jobcentres

Government-run Jobcentres advertise many vacancies each week. Jobs registered at the Jobcentre are normally for unskilled or semi-skilled workers or for clerical and secretarial-level staff, and are usually based in the local area. Even if you are looking for other kinds of work, it is vital to cover every angle, so find out when the new vacancies are released and ensure that you are on the spot when it happens, to be the first in line for an interview should something suitable appear.

It is also worth getting to know staff at Jobcentres. They can offer help and advice on a range of subjects relating to government grants, retraining schemes and special help for those who have been without paid work for a long period and for those with special needs. You may also be able to get legal advice from the Jobcentre on matters relating to employment.

Using your college careers advisory service

If you are about to graduate from a university or college, the careers service is there to help with information and advice.

The service offered by many institutions is also available for use by graduates for up to three years after they have completed their course.

Apart from offering information and careers advice throughout a student's course, the service should also be arranging for companies to visit the institution in their search for graduate employees. Keep an eye on noticeboards or ask the careers advisor for information on the schedule of visits, and make sure that you attend, with a calling card and a perfect CV in hand. Treat these occasions as you would business meetings: make sure you look tidy and serious about finding an entrance to the world of work.

Such visits often take the form of job fairs, at which a number of employers set up their stalls, and give out information about their companies and the opportunities they are offering; or milkround visits, at which companies actively interview candidates.

Many careers services also arrange seminars and short courses on a wide range of general subjects designed to give an insight into the world of work. A further service is the publication of lists of vacancies for those taking finals, those about to finish postgraduate studies and graduates who are available for employment immediately.

All of these services are free and should be utilized to the full. They are specialized services, and the staff running them are expert in placing people with just your qualifications. They probably have good contacts with employers in your field and can be invaluable in your search for work.

Professional registers

Some societies and associations related to specialist areas of work maintain lists of vacancies for their members in much the same way as the student careers advisory service. If you are a member of one of these bodies, it is well worth the phone call to find out if this is the case. Such registers will be open to a very few specialist candidates and so your chances of finding work through one of them is so much greater than the one in 500 chance quoted for applicants responding to advertisements in national newspapers.

If you have a disability of any sort, contact the association that covers your particular case. Again, such institutions often carry lists of vacancies, and may well have one that is suitable for you.

Advertising your availability

While there is a very slim chance of success, advertising your availability for work may bring just the opportunity you need. Research the best place for your advertisement. If you are looking for a local person to employ you as a childminder, perhaps a card in the post office window will bring results. On the other hand, a note in a professional journal may be the way out for a highly-paid specialist. Now that more and more people are going on-line, you might also consider advertising on the Internet. As with all the elements of your search for work, research and common sense should lead you to the right method of publication. And if you are shy about announcing your being without work, there is no need to give your name, just give a box number.

Speculative applications

With so many people chasing each advertised job, it sometimes pays to get ahead of the crowd. The best way to do this is to make personal contact with the people who are hiring in your industry. As previously discussed, a CV presented at a meeting with a friend of a friend could very well bring an offer of work somewhere down the line, but what if you have no mutual friend to link you to the manager you want to work for? What if there are no jobs in your field in your area and you want to move to another? The answer is the written speculative application: writing to employers in the hope that they have an opening coming up that they have not yet advertised, or that they will file your details for future reference. While this is a good way to make contact, do not expect spectacular results. It can also be wasteful of time, effort or money unless you select your target carefully, research it fully and make sure you don't rule yourself out by making a mistake. Here are some pointers:

- Research your targets carefully. A visit to the library will yield a number of business directories that list the names and addresses of companies categorized by the industry they are in. Such directories can give you valuable information about the size of the company (do you want to work in a large or small company?), its profitability (do you want to work for a company that is not doing well?) and the extent and variety of its operations. Make a shortlist of companies that fit your criteria, and then research each one in more detail. Search for articles about them in the indexes to newspapers and magazines:

try the Financial Times index or The Economist. Look back at your old copies of your industry trade publication: any information there? Start a reference file on your target companies. Soon you will build up a picture that either confirms your wish to work for a company or puts you off for life! As with most research jobs, this process will not only give you information for your applications, it will also provide you with material with which to impress your future employer at an interview, and if you eventually start to work for a different company, it will give you plenty of inside information on one of your competitors. You can also add this activity to your list of transferable skills.

- Attend trade fairs and shows related to your field. A simple glance at the catalogue would bring a host of company names to the fore, and a stroll around the stands will give you some idea of what they are all about.
- Find out the name of the person who would hire you, the manager who would be in charge of you if you were to do your job at his company. A simple call to the switchboard may be enough. If you are asked why you are enquiring, say simply that you wish to write to him or her; very few companies will refuse this information without a good reason. If you can, double check you have the right person (the person with the power to hire you) by talking to one of your contacts who works at the company. Keep your eye out for articles in the press that may name new managers. Target them as well: their brief could be to expand their department or replace under-qualified staff.

- Do not send your speculative application to the personnel department. In most companies, personnel staff act as a barrier between applicants and the managers who need the staff. Most personnel staff are so busy sifting applicants for the vacancies they have, that they are not likely to pay much attention to an undirected application. At the same time, personnel staff can be highly critical of applications and may dismiss your letter out of hand if it is not perfect. On the other hand, those people doing the hiring on the whole don't see so many applications and may well have the ten minutes it takes to read your letter and CV and connect you with a role they need to fill.
- On no account should you send a speculative application addressed to 'the manager' or some other job title. It shows you are too lazy to find out who you should be addressing and gives you away as an outsider.
- In your letter, ask for a meeting to discuss the work that is carried out at the company (don't ask directly for a job). Say that you will call about a week later to make an appointment. Make a note in your diary and do it.
- From your first shortlist of companies you may have had a number of meetings, some 'we'll file your CV' letters, but no offer of work. Do not stop there. Leave these irons in the fire and make a fresh start back in the library with the directories, looking for more suitable companies to contact. After a period of about two months, it may be worthwhile going back to your first mailshot targets. Call the switchboard to find out if your previous contact is still in the same job. If not, write to his or her successor (of

course, opening with congratulations on the manager's new appointment). Remind him about your previous contact and tell him what has changed since you were last in touch (perhaps you took a training course or did some temporary work). If the conversation goes well, ask for a meeting.

- In all this process it is vital that your CV is perfect. You are simply wasting a good opportunity if you send out a poor CV, or one that is truthful but does not do you justice for some reason. If you feel this is the case, instead of sending a CV, write a full letter of application describing your experience and asking for a meeting. At the meeting you will need to leave a copy of your CV for the record, but at least you will have had the chance to make a personal impression before the 'facts' can close the door for you. (See pages 75–123 on letters, CVs and application forms.)

- Remember that large companies have a pretty rigid bureaucracy geared towards screening out unsuitable applicants. By contrast, the smaller companies are likely to be more informal about hiring. They usually seem to understand much better than large companies that people are a very important resource and often spend much more time cultivating contacts like you.

- If you have ever had work experience with the company at all, mention it in your letter of application. If you have been told to write to your addressee by a mutual contact, mention it in your letter. If you know you have an experience shared by your addressee (same school, time at the same company, same college, etc.) mention it. Any connection at all between you and the addressee will put you in context and help him get a better idea of who you are.

- If you know you are good on the telephone, or if the job you are looking for requires telephone skills (telesales is the perfect example), you may wish to make contact by phone. Remember, however, that it is easier for the target to say no over the phone, and that you could very quickly rule yourself out. Write a script in advance so that you know what your main selling points are.

- If you have the time and the money to travel, and you have reason to believe there is some chance of success, turn up at the company's office in the hope that the manager (whose name you have already found out) has the time and the inclination to see you. Again, many companies have very efficient receptionists whose job is to act as a barrier between you and the person you are trying to get in to see. Explain politely and clearly that you would like a short meeting to discuss the company's staff requirements. If you ask for ten minutes, don't go over time and don't forget to leave your CV as a calling card. Take with you a copy of your speculative letter of application and your CV in an envelope with the manager's name on it. If she doesn't have time to see you, leave it at reception so that your trip is not entirely wasted. One advantage of making a speculative application in person is that few people like to say no to your face. But cold calling remains very hard work, so think carefully before you undertake it.

Unexpected benefits

Temporary or part-time work should never be ruled out, even if you are looking ultimately for a full-time, permanent job. Temporary and part-time work can get you significant new experience and, if you have been without paid work for a long time, can bring you back into the working world slowly. Many vacancies that arise are filled internally without ever having been advertised publicly, and often the beneficiaries are people who have taken on temporary assignments or part-time work.

Furthermore, in many cases where permanent jobs have been filled by former temporary or part-time staff, both employer and employee have been very satisfied with the outcome. The employee knows what the job involves and has a good idea of the company culture. The employer does not have to rely on the evidence of a CV, a couple of references and first impressions in a short interview for an assessment of the employee. He has in-depth knowledge of the employee's temperament, strengths and weaknesses in advance, something other employers only find out through several months of experience.

If you are a parent returning to work after bringing up a family or someone else returning to the job market after a period of time away, temporary or part-time work is probably just the stepping stone you need to boost your confidence and bring you back into contact with the world of work.

Making work for yourself

If you are a worker with many years' experience behind you, you will have a good idea of what your industry is all about. But if that particular industry wants to make your job obsolete, or has already done so, what are you going to do?

Don't despair. While it is true that older workers are at present less likely to find new jobs once they have lost a job they have held for many years, they also hold the key to helping themselves into a role that is much more exciting and potentially more fulfilling. You know your industry back to front and inside out. You know where your company is doing things wrong and where their competitors are doing things better. You know what companies in your sector need, and more than that you know how to deliver it to them cheaper than the people on the inside. Are you beginning to get the picture?

Making work for yourself is a matter of persuading someone with the power to give you a job that there is a role for you to fill. Most companies have areas of operations in which they could do better. It just takes you to identify what is going wrong and work out how you could be the solution to the problem.

Whether you are going for a full-time job or planning to fill this need as a contractor working on the outside (as many of us will become in the next couple of decades), treat your idea as a business proposal. Be prepared to argue it through from start to finish, giving figures if you can, and aim to prove the following:

- That there is a serious problem that is hindering the company's progress.
- That there is a solution to the problem which could bring a quantifiable improvement in the company's performance in a specified period of time.
- That you are an integral part of the solution, that you can

solve the problem better than they can, and that with you on board there would be measurable benefits.

If you can, have your proposal typed out or turned into a brochure that you can bring to your meetings. Present a well-argued business proposition and you could find yourself back in work tomorrow or moved to a new role not threatened by redundancy as your old one was. Remember that you have a distinct advantage: your experience and inside information.

If you follow the advice in the chapter you have just read, you will be very busy. You certainly cannot say you are without work with all this to do. It is hard work, but it's in the best cause in the world – your own!

GETTING THROUGH

*'The two words 'information' and 'communication' ...
signify quite different things. Information is giving out;
communication is getting through.'*

Sydney J. Harris

The process of selecting an employee is not what it seems. Many applicants believe that the employer is choosing which applicants are the best or the most suitable for the vacancy. In fact, most employers are trying to deselect those applicants who appear unsuitable, leaving a shortlist of people to interview. This may seem a very negative way of going about things, but, when faced with perhaps 500 applicants for one position, it is also effective in getting through the task quickly.

Unless you are known to the employer personally (through your network of contacts, see pages 58–61), you will probably approach him in one of the following ways:

- by sending a CV with a covering letter
- by sending a completed application form
- by sending a letter introducing yourself in the hope that work might become available in the future
- by telephoning

On all these occasions, the employer is trying to find reasons to dismiss your application, so it is worthwhile making sure that you give him no reason to do so, by getting your application skills up to scratch.

This chapter offers advice on compiling a CV, and writing letters and making telephone calls that will not disqualify you at the start of the race.

Meeting the needs of the employer

The candidate who understands that finding a job is all about supply and demand is the one most likely to get somewhere in his search for work. The job-seeker has skills with which to supply the needs of the employer. The task in making contact with the employer is to convince her that you can supply her demand, you can help to solve her problems and fill the gap in her workforce. However, you cannot start to convince her of this until you know exactly what it is she needs.

If you are responding to a situations vacant advertisement, the wording of the advertisement will give you a good, if brief, idea of what the employer is looking for. If you have sent off for an application form (see pages 113–120), the employer may send you some further information. If you are sending a speculative letter (see pages 120–123), you will probably have absolutely no idea what may be on offer: you may even be offered a position you never knew existed but, quite by coincidence, are perfectly qualified to do!

In the case of the speculative application, you will need to be clear what your skills are and show that you are flexible in the kinds of job you are willing to consider. Giving a number of possible job titles will help your contact make the connection between you and a need he has to meet. In the other cases you need to develop the ability to analyse the information you are given and angle your application and your description of yourself so that it is clear that you fit the bill.

Analysing job information

The key to analysing information you have about a particular job is matching the elements required with elements in your own profile. You will also need to divine what problems the employer needs to have solved and decide whether you are able to solve them. One of the easiest ways to do this is to fill in your own form, as if you were screening the job in the same way as the employer will no doubt screen you. The form on pages 80–81 should give you some idea of what you need to find out. If you fill out a form for each position you wish to apply for, you will have a clear record for your research file and, at the end of the exercise, a rating that matches the requirements of the job to your own skills, abilities and desires. You will also have plenty of ammunition for those 'why do you think you are suitable for this job?' questions that we all find difficult to answer (see page 156–63).

The form is designed so that you can list the requirements of the employer against your own selling points. You will see that some of the sections have the words 'preferable' or 'mandatory' next to them. Most employers will tell you what qualifications you must have in order to be considered, and what qualifications would help your application along. They will probably use some of the following terms:

JOB VACANCY PROFILE

Company name _____

Date of advertisement and place _____

Job title _____

	Characteristics Required	**Matching Characteristics**
Qualifications Mandatory	1 _____	_____
	2 _____	_____
	3 _____	_____
Preferred	1 _____	_____
	2 _____	_____
	3 _____	_____
Experience Mandatory	1 _____	_____
	2 _____	_____
	3 _____	_____
Preferred	1 _____	_____
	2 _____	_____
	3 _____	_____
Transferable skills Mandatory	1 _____	_____
	2 _____	_____
	3 _____	_____
Preferred	1 _____	_____
	2 _____	_____
	3 _____	_____

JOB VACANCY PROFILE
Reverse

cont'd	**Characteristics Required**	**Matching Characteristics**
Personal attributes	1 _____	_____
	2 _____	_____
	3 _____	_____
Salary & perks	_____	_____
	_____	_____
Location	_____	_____
	_____	_____
Environment	_____	_____
	_____	_____
Training	_____	_____
	_____	_____
	_____	_____
Prospects	_____	_____
	_____	_____

- ...with at least six GCSEs...
  (mandatory qualification)
- ...life sciences degree an advantage...
  (preferable qualification)
- ...one year's experience in xyz vital...
  (mandatory experience)
- ...solid experience in management important...
  (preferable experience)
- ...show evidence of people management skills...
  (mandatory skill)
- ...fluent French an advantage...
  (preferable skill)

If you are not able to show all the mandatory qualifications listed by the employer, consider how the qualifications you do have could be angled to meet the needs of the employer without being exactly what the employer asks for. If you cannot do this, think twice about applying at all. If you can, make a note that this is not a direct match but an indirect match. You will need to explain in your covering letter why you think you are still suitable even though you are missing a mandatory characteristic.

Very few candidates will fit a job description perfectly. The aim is to approximate the requirements listed as closely as possible. If your experience, qualifications or transferable skills are not quite what is being asked for, try saying to yourself, 'I don't have this, but I do have that, which gives me xyz'. For example, 'I don't have four years experience in retailing, but for ten years I worked in a busy travel agency, which meant I had to deal with the public.' The thinking you have been doing if you read through chapter 1 on assessing your own skills, experience and abilities will help you to match up requirements to attributes.

You will also need to list the characteristics detailed in the advertisement in order of importance. You should be able to tell from the advert what these are, but if not, use your research of the job itself (see page 50–52) to help you deduce a scale of importance.

Do not forget to fill in the information relating to other aspects of the job: salary (is it enough? would you need the car or could you do without it?); location (is it too far away from your home, do you really want to travel so far?); environment (it's all very well wanting to work outside in the summer, but what happens when winter comes?); is training offered? do you need training to advance? do you want a secure job that offers periodical promotion? While it is often tempting to apply to any advertisement that seems suitable, it is important to think of your own needs and desires at this stage as well.

Each time you spot an advertisement that interests you, fill in a Job Vacancy Profile straight away. If you receive further information in the course of your application, draw up a new profile including the new information. The information organized in this way will show you how you will be able to meet the needs of the employer. When you come to write your CV, covering letter and application form, you are already very clear about which parts of your experience you want to highlight and which of your transferable skills the employer is interested in. You will be well on the way to producing an application that proves you are the answer to someone's prayers!

The curriculum vitae

The Latin words 'curriculum vitae' mean 'road of life', and this document is a record of your educational qualifications and employment history. How long a CV is depends on where you are in life. A school-leaver with very little experience of the working world would probably have a single-sheet CV, while a freelance consultant who has been working for 30 years may run to two or even three sides, particularly if she wishes to use the third page to list her clients or name and describe various prestigious projects undertaken. CVs are difficult documents to compile. Expect to spend some time drafting and redrafting yours until you have the balance of information right, and until you are certain that you are giving a clear picture, using readable grammar, correct spelling and logical layout.

Some people are tempted to use a bureau to compile their CV. The service most often includes drafting and typing your CV to a standard format using the information you give them on a form. A good service can be very expensive, but the professional presentation of the end result could be just the edge you need. However, no-one knows your strengths and weaknesses as well as you do, and if you have worked your way through chapter 1 (see pages 7–26), you should have all the material you need to put your own CV together. If you are worried about your spelling or grammar letting you down, find someone you know to have good writing skills (it could be a friend, spouse or mentor [see page 45], for example) and ask him or her to help you correct the draft. While your helper is doing this, ask also if he or she can give you some feedback on what you have chosen to include and the overall picture you are putting across.

A CV is intended as an outline only, but it will probably also be used by the potential employer as a starting point for questions in the interview, so when making an initial list of items you wish to include, consider how they may provoke questions, and how you might respond. Try to anticipate problem areas that may be embarrassing to explain, or that might prejudice your chances.

There are two types of CV commonly in use. The standard CV gives not much more than the bare facts. It lists jobs, schools, qualifications and interests in a pretty dispassionate way. It is useful to follow the usual format and order of sections in the standard CV, because many employers are used to looking at this format and may become irritated if they are sent a CV that is organized in some other way. It is easier to find information in a format the reader recognizes, than in an unfamiliar layout.

However, the standard CV can show up all sorts of warts: periods of unemployment, a shorter than usual list of academic qualifications, a chequered career, a candidate who is too old or too young. Other methods of giving the same information can make you seem more dynamic and can highlight the details you want the employer to take note of, for example, varied work experience rather than poor exam results, a recent refresher course and a handful of transferable skills rather than ten years 'without work' while you brought up a family of four.

It is up to you which of the following two formats you use for your CV. You may even want to use different formats for different occasions: the standard CV to be sent out in reply to advertisements, and the skills-orientated CV to be left with a contact after a meeting, for example.

The standard CV

The standard CV is the document that most of us recognize. It is the format that employers expect to see when they ask for a CV to be sent with a covering letter. The information is given in blocks under the following headings:

- Personal details
- Statement of objectives
- Education
- Vocational training and qualifications
- Work experience
- Skills
- Personal interests
- References

Personal details

Give your full name, address and contact numbers, including postcodes and dialling codes. If your CV is going to an employer abroad, perhaps to a country in which it is usual to reverse the family name and the given name, underline your family name. If you have honours (a degree or membership of a professional body, for example), give the initials to which you are entitled after your name: Karen Jones BFA (Hons); John Neil MChl; Adrian Moore BSc, MICE.

If you are between addresses, or have a home address and a business or term-time address, give both and label them clearly so that the employer knows how to get hold of you at any time. Of course, if you don't want a potential employer to telephone you at work (perhaps you have not yet informed your employer that you are looking for another job), don't give your telephone number at work.

It was once standard practice to give your date of birth and age, and most employers still like to have an idea of how old you are. However, if you think your age may disqualify you (either you think you may be too old or too young), leave this information out. Only give your age if you know that you are without doubt the right age for the job.

Also, some employers look for an indication of marital status. There is absolutely no need for an employer to know what your family arrangements are, and, again, information of this type can lead to discrimination, so do not volunteer it on your CV. However, if you feel you absolutely must, use the terms 'single' or 'married'. If you are divorced, use 'single'; if you are separated, use 'married'. This avoids the connotations of instability and emotional upheaval that the words 'divorced' and 'separated' bring with them.

Statement of objectives

This is a short paragraph, normally of no more than one or two sentences, in which you state your aim in making the application (to take on greater responsibility, for example, or to find new challenges, exercise other skills, work in a new field). Looking back at the notes you made when reading chapter 1 on defining your own needs (page 23–6), you should be able to put together a concise statement of this sort. When replying to advertisements for particular positions, your aim is to make it sound as if you are looking for the kind of position that is on offer by tailoring your description of your own needs to the employer's description of the job. This does not mean that you should say that you want qualities in the job that you would hate, simply that you relate your statement of objectives to the advertisement in some way. See pages 76–7 for more on tailoring your application to the requirements of the employer.

Education

This section is usually made up of a chronological list of educational institutions and studies, including qualifications gained. Give the following information:

- Names and locations of schools attended at secondary level, giving dates of attendance.
- Qualifications gained, including grades for the latest qualifications only (i.e. if you have 'A'-levels but also a degree, give the grade of the degree only). If your degree is not of the simple single-subject variety, you may need to explain and list the major studies you undertook.

The reader is probably eager to spend as little time as possible going over CVs, and so will stop reading yours at any point if he becomes bored or irritated. If you list your negative points first, he may have discounted yours even before he gets to your excellent work record. Therefore, if your school performance or academic record is not as good as it might be, shuffle the order of your CV so that your work experience comes first. In this way, the employer should read of your more positive points first, before getting to the negative parts. In general, try to get your good points on the first page of the CV, or in the upper two thirds of a one-page document. See pages 106 for more notes on layout.

Vocational training and qualifications

Give a chronological list of the other training courses you have attended and qualifications gained (if any). Give the following information:

- The name of the course and duration (if more than one week).
- Dates attended.
- Qualifications gained (if appropriate).
- The trainer: if this is a well-known body, its reputation could add to the perceived value of your training.

Work experience

List in chronological or reverse chronological order your employment, giving:

- Employer's name and location.
- Dates of employment.
- Employer's business if this is not obvious.
- Your position (if you went through two or more different positions, list all of them separately and group the responsibilities relevant to each under that particular title, showing a clear progression up the ladder of

experience and responsibility.

- Short description of responsibilities, including such information as number of staff supervised, tasks undertaken, goals attained, targets met, your achievements while in the job. Do not give reasons for leaving: these can be discussed at the interview if the employer is interested.

Advisors are divided as to whether a person should mention periods of 'unemployment'. Of course, as the face of work changes so that fewer and fewer people have unbroken work records, and employers begin to understand the importance and value of 'unpaid work' or work that is undertaken outside a perceptible career structure, periods without paid work will no longer count against applicants. Meanwhile, as most recruiters still look for periods of time not accounted for in CVs, it is advisable to include periods of unemployment.

If you do decide to label your periods of unemployment, write about them in a positive way. Describe your job-seeking activities in professional terms:

May 1991–August 1992 Employment break
Researched job market in xyz field. Devised and operated research filing and contact tracking system. Developed writing and analysis skills. Improved spoken French skills at conversation classes.

Let the employer know that even though you were not being

paid, you were actively using and developing skills just as if you were in employment.

Skills
This section comprises a list of your transferable skills (see page 19). Include such abilities as: driving, typing and shorthand speeds, foreign languages of which you have a working knowledge or in which you are fluent, knowledge of computer software, ability to operate certain types of machinery, ability to write reports, public speaking, knowledge of filing systems, negotiating skills, etc.

Personal interests
A list of the activities you take part in when not at work, such as a certain kind of sport or a certain form of cooking. Try to list at least three or four activities. Perhaps more than half a dozen activities is excessive (the employer may think you cannot possibly have time to do *all* those things in depth). Try also to make the list as specific as possible. Avoid saying 'Reading, arts, sport, travel'. Define each activity clearly. Show that you have chosen to specialize, that you have exercized some discretion: 'reading modern fiction'; 'modern abstract art'; 'I play football regularly', 'travel in Spanish-speaking countries, particularly Latin America'.

It is usual for more experienced people to drop this section from their CVs, particularly if they are simply using the document as an *aide-mémoire* for the potential client. Again, be prepared to discuss any or all of the interests you have listed and don't embroider: real connoisseurs of Argentinian dessert wines could be lurking in the most unexpected places, and according to Murphy's Law are most likely to be sitting behind the interviewer's desk!

Referees

Most people give the names and addresses of two people who have agreed to act as referees. If you give contact details on your CV, however, the employer could contact your referees without telling you that he is considering you for the position. To avoid this happening, and to protect the privacy of your referees, simply indicate that references are available on request.

It is usual to ask potential referees for permission to give their names, and to thank them when they have given a reference, even if you did not get the job. You might also double-check at this stage whether your referee feels able to give a good reference! Referees have a duty to be truthful, so most would probably decline your request if they felt they would have to say something that might prejudice your chances of a job.

The custom is to choose one referee who knows you well in a personal aspect, and has some standing in the community. That person may be a member of the clergy, a local business person or politician, a schoolteacher or college tutor. It is important that your personal referee has known you for some time and can therefore speak from long experience. The employer would expect the reference to contain information about character and behaviour.

The second referee should ideally be your most recent

employer, or a person who has direct experience of you at work and so is well placed to speak about your professional conduct and abilities. The well-connected applicant will choose somebody who is well known in the industry or perhaps known to the potential employer. The key to a successful reference is to find someone who can speak with authority and relevance to your needs.

Examples of a standard CV

The standard CVs on pages 92 and 94–5 could have been put together, first by a young man about to leave school and looking for his first job and second by a woman in her early thirties who wants to develop further in her career.

What to miss out

Unless you are specifically asked to do so, do not include any reference to your religion, race or political persuasion (this includes membership of pressure groups). Differences on these fronts are (illegal or not) a sure-fire way to get your CV rejected at the first round.

Do not mention any disability that might encourage a potential employer to dismiss your application. If you have not already been interviewed, your aim is to avoid being deselected in the first round – you will have a much better chance of persuading the employer that your disability does not stop you doing the job if you are talking to her face to face.

You may feel quite strongly that this is unfair or dishonest. However, look at it from another angle. We all have handicaps of some sort or another. We could be talking about a person's

Curriculum Vitae

Name:	Damien Halliday
Address:	26 Farmer's Court
	Oxleigh
	OX3 8TB
Telephone:	(01234) 5678901

Objective

To secure an entry-level position in electrical engineering that combines vocational training, direct shop-floor experience and good promotion prospects.

Education

1990–1994 Oxleigh Comprehensive School, Oxleigh
Qualifications: 8 GCSEs

Physics (B)	Mathematics (B)
Design and Technology (B)	German (B)
Chemistry (C)	Geography (C)
History (C)	English (D)

Skills

Working knowledge of German. Basic keyboard skills.

Employment

1993–present Goodfood Hamburgers Ltd, Oxleigh
Position: counter assistant. Weekend job taking food orders and serving customers. Won Assistant-of-the-Month Award three months running.

Personal Interests

Reading science fiction; maintaining and using home computer system; member of Oxleigh Rugby Club.

References

Available on request.

inability to handle people, or to work competently with numbers or undertake presentations or write reports or a fear of heights, flying, water. Those with psychological or emotional handicaps have the advantage of those with physical handicaps in that the disabilities of the former are invisible. Those with invisible handicaps don't mention them in applications, so why should those with visible handicaps? What matters is whether we allow our disabilities to stop us doing what we want to do. If you have a physical disability and are applying for jobs, it is clear that you have decided not to let your disability get in the way, so do not put yourself at a disadvantage. Your aim is to get into the interview room and to give yourself the opportunity to overcome the matter of your difference when you meet the employer face to face.

The skills-orientated CV

An alternative format is used when you want to highlight the transferable skills you have, rather than your education or work history. This is particularly useful when you have done a number of unrelated jobs and want to bring all the skills information into one clear picture of yourself. As mentioned earlier, it can also play down any problems with broken work record, long or several periods of unemployment or lack of academic qualifications.

Career summary

The skills-orientated CV starts in the normal way with name, address and contact telephone numbers (home and work if applicable) but omitting the words Curriculum Vitae at the

Curriculum Vitae

Jane Harris

PERSONAL DETAILS

Address:	69 Elmtree Gardens
	Enderby
	CV23 4ZZ
Telephone:	(01234) 5678901
Date of Birth:	16th October 1963
Nationality:	British
	Full British driver's licence

OBJECTIVE To secure a new position in publications in which to continue my contact with France and French, but also to develop my knowledge of the publishing process towards a senior role that brings wider responsibilities.

EDUCATION

1976–1981	Enderby Grammar School
	9 GCE 'O'-Levels
	4 GCE 'A'-Levels
1981	Language Insitute
	Introduction to TEFL
1982–1985	Hartham University
	BA (Hons) Contemporary Studies Class 2:2
1985–1986	Leggatt College, Grantby
	Bi-lingual secretarial studies

EMPLOYMENT

1981–1982	St Cecilia School, Noumea, New Caledonia
	English assistant: taught school pupils aged 14–18

1986–1987	Fontainebleu SA, London Secretary to the publishing director: general secretarial duties; document translation, interpreting, liaison with counterparts in parent company in France.
1987–1990	Pan-Europe Publications Ltd, London Secretary to international sales director, business publications: preparation of sales documents in English and French; planned international sales trips and interpreted at meetings; handled correspondence, daily secretarial tasks.
1990–present	Anglo-French Institute, London Publications officer: administered the translation of brochures, leaflets and other documents from English to French and French to English. Liaised with production department on design, production and printing. Wrote a number of documents. Promoted to senior publications officer in 1994.
SKILLS	Fluent French; conversant with Apple Macintosh word-processing systems; some knowledge of Apple Macintosh DTP systems.

PERSONAL INTERESTS

French films, cooking, playing squash (secretary of the Enderby squash league); reading modern fiction in French and English.

start. The next section is a career summary. Like the statement of objectives, the career summary is a one- or two-sentence encapsulation of the most important selling points of the following CV. It should tell the reader immediately what is unique about you. It will probably read rather like an advertisement for a lonely hearts column:

'Ambitious team leader with strong organization and motivation skills and a proven track record in telephone sales'

'Charismatic communications manager with PR background, eight years' management experience and excellent people skills'

'Professionally qualified legal secretary with fluent French and good organization skills'

'Indefatigable nursery nurse with 25 years' experience in private service in Europe and the United States'

The exact words you choose should relate to the description of the ideal candidate given in the advertisement (if there is one). (See pages 77–81). You may wish to leave the career summary until last when compiling your CV: then you will have a much better idea of the 'angle' you want to highlight, the spin you want to put on your career story.

Transferable skills

This section lists all the skills you think are strongest, and which you would like to 'sell'. Make sure that all the skills mentioned in the advertisement (if there is one) are included. It is probably best to write this as a list of bullet points rather than as a paragraph of full sentences; the list format encourages you to be more economical with words and is quicker and easier to read:

- Fluent in French, working knowledge of Spanish and Italian
- Proficient with Macintosh systems including x, y and z software packages
- Familiarity with all common office equipment including fax, photocopier, modem, etc.
- Familiarity with paper filing systems and research techniques
- Strong interpersonal skills
- Conscientious self-starter with initiative and attention to detail
- Clean driver's licence with Advanced Driver's Certificate

Order your skills so that those most apposite to the work you are seeking come first and those least relevant, but still important, come last. Your list should be about six points long.

In an interview, you will probably be asked to explain and give examples that prove each of the points you have listed, so make sure that your claims can be backed up with a good illustration of that skill in use.

Career development

Give the name and location of the employer as for the standard CV (see pages 87–8), give your job-title and a list of the tasks you fulfilled. Include in this list your achievements while in this particular job. Try to quantify each achievement so that it stands on its own and so that the reader understands where the success lay. Most employers would be interested in activities that improve business or solve problems: increasing sales, profitability or efficiency, reducing staff turnover, tackling poor time-keeping, absenteeism, low productivity, to name but a few. So if you can say that you have dealt successfully with any of these problems or others, the employer will soon begin to think what problems you could solve for her. Here are more examples:

- Developed a completely new sales region in the face of established competition, achieving £165,000 turnover in the first six months and tripling that figure by the end of that year.
- Set up and monitored new mail room system, involving the recruitment of four new staff and the purchase of £50,000-worth of new equipment.
- Won Assistant-of-the-Month Award three months running.
- Brought in three xyz projects consecutively, on time and under budget.
- Developed relationships between warehousing and transport departments.
- Controlled a budget of more than £600,000.

Education, training and qualifications

List your qualifications, giving school or college, subject and date as for the standard CV. If you have a further or higher education qualification, there is no need to list the subjects or grades of GCSEs or A-levels, apart from giving the number of qualifications at this level. Use this section also to include courses related to your work that you have undertaken.

Personal details/Personal achievements

In this part of your CV you have a choice. You could add a section titled 'Personal Details', and list your non-professional activities as for the standard CV (see page 89). However, your CV will seem more dynamic if you angle the section slightly differently, by giving a list of achievements that do not fall into your professional development under the title 'Personal Achievements':

- Taught English as a foreign language to adult students in Sri Lanka, achieving a 92% pass rate at 'A'-level.
- Represented the county at the national athletics championship in 1995.
- Achieved Grade 6 piano with merit within two years of taking up the instrument.
- Formed the Hadleston Centenary Association, organizing a series of 25 fund-raising events during the town's centenary year. Raised nearly £16,000 for the Residents' Trust.
- In 1996, cycled from x to y (xxx miles in xxx days) in aid of charity.

In this section you might also include membership of national, professional or academic bodies. However, if you prefer to use the 'Personal Details', you could use this space to include date of birth, marital status (if wanted), health, personal interests and anything else you feel is relevant.

On pages 102–3 there is an example of a skills-orientated CV.

Tips for a winning CV

It is not only the content of your CV that could deny you the chance of an interview. You might destroy your chances with a couple of spelling mistakes, verbose writing style poor layout. Here are some tips to help you avoid this catastrophe.

- **First person singular**

  Even in a CV – the only document dedicated to talking about oneself – using the first person pronoun (I) can become wearing to the reader. Some people avoid this by adopting a telegraphic style: 'I managed a team of five' becomes 'Managed a team of five', for example. Others use the third person throughout as if they were talking about someone else: 'She managed a team of five'. The first solution is more widely used, but whichever you opt for, make sure that you use it consistently throughout the document, and avoid switching from 'I managed', to 'Managed', to 'She managed', which is just hopelessly confusing.

- **Check your spelling**

  On no account should you rely on a computer spelling-checker to correct your spelling. Most of these programmes are written by Americans, whose spelling is often different from standard UK English. Spelling checkers also miss instances in which the word sounds the same but is spelled differently to the word you should be using (homonyms): where and wear, for example, or weather and whether, or their, there and they're. Use a dictionary. If you don't own one, buy one! Never send out a finished CV unless it has been read by at least one person other than yourself. However good your spelling may be, there may be one error that you simply did not see, and that one error could cost you an interview. Make sure particularly that you spell correctly the words used in the advertisement (if there is one). If your English is not good, enroll in a class at your local adult education centre where you will find that learning later in life is not at all as bad as when you were at school as a child. Good English skills are an investment that will pay dividends for the rest of your life. (You may even meet someone who knows someone who has just the job for you!)

- **Jargon and technical terms**
  If you must use technical terms and jargon in your CV, make sure that you are using them correctly, and that they are terms used widely in your field. Unless they really are in the mainstream, avoid using abbreviations and acronyms: computer-aided design is better than CAD, but RSPCA and BBC are acceptable. This all comes down to who you are addressing with your CV and how much you expect them to understand about the work experience, skills and qualifications you are presenting.
- **Keep it short and avoid clichés**

John Cowley
26 Mildmay Court
Coventry CV89 4ZZ
Telephone/fax: (01234) 5678901

Bilingual book sales professional with particular experience
in African markets and proven skills in market development

Skills

- Strong negotiator and communicator

- Fluent French and 5 years' experience of African
  francophone markets

- In-depth knowledge of the market for educational books in Africa

- Excellent organization, time-management and training skills

Career development

1991–present Books for Education Ltd, education publishers

Sales representative – Africa team

- Negotiated sales of French language educational titles in all
  Francophone sub-Saharan African countries

- Achieved 10% increase in sales to the region in the first year

- Reduced costs by 20% by sourcing new transportation suppliers

- Set up and manned office in Abidjan (Côte d'Ivoire) before training
  resident staff and eventually handing over

1986–1991 Edward Blake & Sons, trade publishers

Travelling sales representative, northern region

- Maintained sales with existing clients

- Developed new bookshop business

- Successfully introduced the company's reference list to non-traditional outlets such as stationery shops

- Increased regional sales by 35% in the first two years and by a steady 10% in successive years

- Produced monthly sales reports

- Liaised with central warehousing and marketing staff

Education, training and qualifications

1986 Mildmay University
BA (Hons)
Modern Languages: French and Portuguese. Grade: 2:1

1990 Make that Deal! One-week (residential) course at Forum Business College, London

1992 Started part-time modular degree in African studies: four out of eight modules attained so far (Open All Hours Adult Studies College)

Use one word where you are tempted to use two. Write in short sentences with one sentence covering one point. Do not try to say too much. Avoid clichés that sound good but mean nothing. Plain English is better than pseudo-technical language. Use active and positive words to describe what you have done and can do. See pages 14 for a list of words you might like to call on.

- **Keep your layout clear**

  Use headings highlighted in bold or underlined to mark the different sections of your CV. If you have a choice, use a clear, unfussy typestyle. Avoid using italic typestyles, most of which are difficult to read. Times (the style designed for the newspaper) is often available, and is clear and easy to read, making it a good standard.

- **Use lists**

  Lists of information are quick to read and easier to digest than paragraphs of full sentences. You will probably be able to get more onto one sheet using lists.

- **Presentation**

  Produce your CV on good quality plain A4 paper. Do not use coloured paper (which does not copy well) and do not use patterned paper. If you intend to photocopy the CV many times, keep a master in a file where it will not become dog-eared. It will also help to have a copy when you come to update your CV. Never photocopy a copy. This will give poor quality. Use a good typewriter or word processor. If you have to, go to an agency that specializes in typing documents. Do not settle for second best in the presentation stakes. Never send out a handwritten CV.

It pays to keep your CV up to date. Keep notes on your achievements in your current job and make a record of new qualifications as you attain them. Date your CVs so that you know when each was written.

Covering letters

The covering letter is used to accompany and introduce your CV (or application form) when sending it to an employer. It should say what prompted the applicant to write and point out the merits of the application.

Keep it short. The longer your letter, the more chance there is that you will say something detrimental to your cause. Selectors do not have time to read long rambling letters, and will probably be irritated by them.

The covering letter should be laid out as a standard business letter on A4 paper, preferably the same as the paper used for your CV. Particularly if requested to do so in an advertisement, write the covering letter by hand. Use a good-quality pen to improve your handwriting and put the sheet of paper over a pad of lined paper so that you have the lines to guide you and keep yours straight. If your handwriting is poor you may resent constantly being asked to write letters by hand. However, employers hardly ever ask for something that they do not consider vital to their selection process. First, clear handwriting is considered to be a measure of tidiness in your mental life. Second, some large companies make use of graphology (the study of handwriting) to find out more about you and will therefore want a specimen. If your handwriting really is so bad, perhaps it is worth picking up a book from the library on how you can improve it. Calligraphy classes at a local adult education centre could also indirectly improve your normal handwriting.

Do not allow your letter to go out with blots, alterations or crossings out, and don't resort to the use of liquid paper. It must be spotless. Take the time to make your application count.

Never, never send a CV with a photocopied form letter in which the body of the letter is the same each time, but you have to fill the gaps with the specific information. Form letters of this type have all but disappeared from the business world and will stick out like a sore thumb. Equally, if you are sending out form letters, you are not tailoring your application towards each particular vacancy. You may think form letters save time, but they just lose you vital opportunities.

Structure of the covering letter

The standard structure is as follows:

- writer's address (top right-hand corner or top centred, never top left).
- date (left-hand side below the level of the writer's address).
- recipient's name, position and address (left-hand side starting below the date).
- salutation (Dear Mr X, etc.)
- paragraph one: introduction, putting the application in context
- paragraph two: highlighting relevant skills and experience
- paragraph three: asking for action

- complimentary close: (Yours sincerely, etc.)
- signature and signatory details

Writer's address
Give your full address, including the full postcode, and add your telephone, mobile phone, fax, modem, pager or other contact details. These should be the same as those given on your CV.

Date
Make sure that you are writing on the day of the advertisement if possible. If not, and you are writing only a couple of days after the advertisement date, give that date anyway: people hardly ever check the post mark on envelopes, and if you give a later date you may seem to have lagged behind the crowd.

Recipient's name, position and address
Copy these exactly from the advertisement. Make no mistakes in spelling: many people take mistakes in the pronunciation or spelling of their name as a personal insult. Many advertisements give the position of the recruiter instead of her name. If this is the case, call the advertiser's office to find out the name and title of the person who will be dealing with the recruitment. Always avoid writing to a position if you can. If you do have a name, include the job title as well. This is because people go on holiday or leave their jobs without warning. If this is the case the letter with a reference to the position will be dealt with by the next person to hold that

position (at least in well-organized companies), and your application has less chance of going astray.

In most large companies with personnel departments, it is the personnel staff who make up the initial shortlist of applicants for interview. The person who actually hires the staff is the manager who will ultimately be responsible for them. Therefore, if you are in the happy circumstance of knowing the hiring manager, send your CV to him directly. (The only question this raises is: why have you not been aware of this vacancy before the advertisement was published? If you have made good use of your contacts you should have heard of it long ago.) As a precaution, however, send an application to personnel also.

Salutation
Never use a person's Christian name in the salutation unless that is all you are given in the advertisement. Always start Dear Mrs, Ms, Mr or Dear Sir or Madam (if you want to be particularly formal or cannot discover the name of the person doing the recruiting).

Paragraph one
Tell the addressee where you saw the advertisement or heard of the vacancy. Say that you would like to apply and that you are enclosing your CV:

> 'I read your advertisement for an experienced fitter in today's *Pockwick Herald*. I would like to apply for the position and enclose my curriculum vitae as requested.'

'I would like to apply for the position of retail assistant advertised in today's *Pockwick Herald* (reference SA/PH 8.8.96).'

Keep it to one or two sentences if you can. Avoid starting with 'I am writing...'. Of course you are writing – that's obvious and a waste of words. Give the job title (copied from the advertisement) and any reference. Some companies advertise a number of jobs at once and so it is useful to let the employer know which job you are applying for straight away. Some advertisements ask that you state the position and job reference. If this is the case, do not miss them out.

Paragraph two
Use the next paragraph to point out any experience and skills that are particularly relevant given the description in the advertisement. If possible, use the exact words that the advertiser has used and confirm that you have the qualities required in the order of the advertisement.

'Wanted: Lively receptionist/secretary with xyz word-processing package, excellent typing and telephone manner. Must be able to work on own initiative and be well-groomed. Second jobber. Non-smoking office outside town.'

The applicant responding to this advertisement might compose a second paragraph along these lines.

'As you will see from my enclosed CV, I have two years' experience using xyz word-processing package and have achieved a typing speed of 90 words per minute. My present job requires a well-groomed appearance and good telephone manner. I do not smoke and live very close to your office, so would have no problem with transport.'

Use this paragraph too to overcome areas in which you do not match the advertisement's requirements.

'While this would not be my second but my third job, I would be moving into a different industry and so would need to consolidate my skills in the same way as a second jobber would.'

'Your advertisement asks for five years' experience in a management role, and as you will see, I have only three years as manager. However, for the preceding four years I deputized regularly for the manager and so have long experience of management skills and responsibilities.'

By doing this you are showing the employer that you have thought about the position and made the conscious decision that you would be suitable for the job, rather than throwing your application into the post without really considering what the position would involve.

Paragraph three

This paragraph should round off your letter and state your position. At this stage what you want more than anything else is an interview. Ask for this politely and confidently. Invite positive action.

> 'I hope that we will be able to meet to discuss this position.'

> 'I hope that you consider my application suitable, and look forward to arranging to meet you.'

> 'I would very much like to meet you to discuss this vacancy, and would be able to attend a meeting at your convenience.'

Avoid such clichés as 'Thank you in advance for your kind attention,' the wishy-washy 'I look forward to hearing from you', and the grovelling 'I hope you will consider my application worthy of a response.'

Complimentary close

Use 'Yours sincerely' if your salutation gave the person's name (i.e. Dear Mr Jones). Use 'Yours faithfully' if you addressed a hypothetical person only (i.e. Dear Sir). Never use the less formal and more intimate formulas: best regards, kind regards, or best wishes. These are much too familiar for this context, and should be reserved for letters to colleagues you know well, or friends and acquaintances.

Signature and signatory details

Sign using your normal signature. Try to develop a signature that is neat and stylish, but lacks unnecessary flourishes that may make you seem immature.

If your signature is illegible, write your name in capital letters underneath. Add the letters Enc. (for a one-sheet CV) and Encs (for a multiple sheet CV). This indicates that there are enclosures in the envelope.

Layout for letters

There are two styles of layout in common use: semi-blocked and fully-blocked. The fully-blocked style (in which paragraphs have line spaces between them instead of indented first lines) is now almost universally used for business correspondence, so if you choose to type your letter, this style is best. An example of a letter laid out in the fully-blocked style is given on page 122.

If you are handwriting your letter, however, you have a choice of either style, although even in handwritten letters, the semi-blocked layout has started to look dated. An example of a letter laid out in semi-blocked style is given on page 114.

Faxing your CV

Some advertisers ask you to fax your CV if you have the facilities. You may consider doing this anyway to get ahead of the pack. If you do fax your covering letter and CV, compile the covering letter in the same way as usual, but adding the fax number to the recipient's address. At the end, replace the abbreviation Encs with an indication of the number of pages in the fax: '2 pages follow' is a good formula. Number your pages (starting with your letter) so that if the machine fails to send one your recipient knows which one she is missing. Put the covering letter and the CV in the post that day to give the recipient a fair copy for the file.

Questions of salary

Some recruiters ask that you give them an indication of your current salary or of what salary you would require to do the job. *Never* tell the recruiter what you are currently earning. Give instead a well-researched salary range for the job (see pages 134–5) and say that this is negotiable depending on the final job description and the other elements in the employment package:

> 'You ask in your advertisement for an indication of salary requirements. I would need a salary of between £15,000 and £17,500, depending on the exact requirements of the position and other elements of the package being offered.'

An example of a covering letter is given on pages 116. *Collins Pocket Reference Letter Writing*, published in the same series as this book, gives more detailed information and advice on writing letters, which should be particularly useful if you are unfamiliar with common business practice.

Application forms

There are many instances in which you may be asked to fill out

26 Priory Park Crescent,
Brigston BR1 1EE
Telephone/Fax: (01234) 5678901

16th March 1997

Mr S Neale,
Publicity Manager,
Pockwick Publicity Ltd,
24 Pockwick Road,
Pockwick PW3 2TY

Dear Mr Neale,

I read with interest your advertisement for a press and publications officer in today's Pockwick Herald and would ask you to consider my curriculum vitae, which is enclosed.

You will see that I have two years' experience in PR, and in that time have developed a wide range of contacts at both local and national level. I have exceptional communication and administration skills, coupled with vitality and drive. I am looking to widen my experience into publications and it seems that this position would allow me to do so.

If you consider my application suitable, I would be most happy to meet you at your convenience to discuss the vacancy further.

Yours sincerely,

Jane David
Encs

an application form for a job. If you visit a recruitment consultancy and employment agency you will probably be asked to do so as a matter of routine, and many employers are now doing the same.

Personnel staff and others involved in selection prefer to use application forms because they make each applicant give the same information in the same order as all the others. This makes it easier for staff to analyse large numbers of applications quickly. It can also help you by ensuring that you include all the information necessary in a format that is easy for the reader to follow.

If an advertisement asks that you send for a form and fill it in, do exactly that. Do not send your CV with a covering letter and do not return the application form incomplete with 'see CV attached' written across it. If the employer wants to see an application form then it is polite to fill one in, and it is job-seeking suicide to do anything else. Always carry a copy of your CV to interviews (particularly spur-of-the-moment calls on employment agencies). You never know when you will be asked to fill in an application form and your CV will act as a useful crib sheet for you.

It may, however, serve some purpose to send your CV along with a completed application form, particularly if it highlights strengths and experience you feel you have not been given space to mention in the form. If you decide to do this, staple the CV to the form to stop them becoming separated.

Requesting an application form

This usually necessitates a phone call (often to a machine) or a short letter. Treat both of these as if you were in contact with the person who will be interviewing you – you probably are! Even telephone answering machines are monitored by people, possibly people with the power to throw your application out, and a mumbling and confused message will give a very poor first impression. Speak clearly (write a script for yourself if you think you are going to get nervous) and spell any names that might give trouble.

If you are asked to send off for an application form, observe all the rules for covering letters (pages 105–112). The following form of words is acceptable:

> 'With reference to your advertisement for counter staff in today's *Clerkston Herald*, I would be grateful if you would send an application form. I am enclosing a stamped addressed envelope.'

There is no need to labour over this letter. Keep it to one paragraph if you can. Remember to check for spelling errors. Some employers ask that you enclose a stamped, self-addressed envelope, and if this is the case make sure that you do not forget. Put a first class stamp on both envelopes or you will lose the advantage of speed.

Making a start
When you receive your application form, you will probably also receive information about the position advertised and you should study this carefully before making a start. Use all the techniques covered in the section on analysing job

advertisements (pages 77–81) to work out what kind of person the advertiser is looking for and ensure that your application shows that you fit the bill.

You should make two drafts of your application in rough before touching the actual form, the first on ordinary paper and the second on a photocopy of the form. Make this second version as close as you can to the version you send to the employer: this will be your file copy as well as your double check that it is possible to say everything you want to say in the space allotted.

Keeping copies of all your applications, not only application forms, is a good idea. You will be able to refresh your memory as to what you said in your application the night before your interview, and previous applications can give you ideas as to how to answer questions on the one in hand. But do not simply copy the information given on one application form over to another: each employer asks questions in a slightly different way, and each job requires different characteristics to be highlighted.

Before you start writing, read the form from start to finish. Note any instructions and follow them to the letter. Answer all the questions, and fill in all the space given, not with large handwriting, but with information about how you fit the bill. Make sure that your writing is neither too cramped nor too loose. Look at how much space is allocated for each question. From this you will be able to work out which parts of the form are the most important. Add extra sheets only if this is suggested on the form itself, and avoid the temptation to use this as an excuse to waffle.

Use black ink, not blue, red or any other colour unless asked to do so on the form. This is because black ink gives the best photocopies. If you are an accomplished typist you may like to type your application, but, again, watch for instructions that tell you you must fill it in by hand.

Handling application form questions

The questions on application forms usually fall into two categories: questions that require factual answers (lists of schools, colleges, qualifications, jobs, medical details, etc.); and those that require a short essay-style answer.

Many people do badly at the latter type of question. They are not clear what they should be writing, they do not plan their 'essay' and they do not answer the question being asked. By asking such questions, employers are trying to find out what you think the job entails and what strengths and experiences you would be able to bring to it. This is your chance to highlight your selling points. Attack the question as if you were writing a covering letter:

- In what ways does your work experience match with the job description?
- Does this job offer you something you are looking for? A chance to use certain skills? To consolidate experience? To move into a slightly different area? To move from part-time to full-time work? Go back to the notes you made on the kind of person you are and what you want from life and from your next job; there should be plenty of inspiration there.

- Does the employer have any problems that you could solve? Show that you have the skills to do so.

When working out your answer remember that these questions above all others will be used to provoke conversation in interviews, so try to imagine how you would handle that conversation.

Smile please!

A few recruiters like to see what the candidate looks like. This is obviously important if you are an actor or model, for instance, but is less important, and possibly even questionable, for other kinds of work.

However, if you are asked for a photograph, you should send one, if only to avoid being discounted because you omitted to do so. Do not under any circumstances send a holiday snap of you and your friend Barbara on the beach! Have professional photographs taken if you can afford to, or go to a studio that offers while-you-wait passport photos. Have your pictures shot in black and white. While slightly more expensive than colour, black and white portraits are more stylish and much more likely to do you justice. Avoid photo booths where possible. The results from such machines are of good enough quality for some purposes, but not for job applications.

Covering letters for application forms

It is standard business practice to send some explanation with any correspondence. Companies use compliments slips to do this when there is nothing to say other than here is the item you wanted. In the same way, when you send an application form back, you should write a short covering letter. Follow the guidelines on pages 105–112.

Speculative applications

A speculative application is one sent to a company that has not advertised a vacancy. You are speculating that the company needs someone with your skills and experience and are making contact in the hope that this is the case, or that the least the company will do is put your details on file for future reference. Contractors and freelancers will be used to doing this, but those more used to being employed by someone else will need to learn the skills involved.

You should send a CV with a covering letter, but without researching which employers to target, you will be whistling in the wind.

If you have followed the advice in chapter 3 on researching possible employers and seeking out personal contacts, you will already know the details of the companies that employ people with your skills (or may do so in the future), and you should have already found out who in particular has the power to hire you. Direct your application to this member of staff personally. If possible, find someone whose name you can use in your letter: 'John Bean suggested I contact you' is a good first line if John Bean happens to be a colleague on good terms with the person you are writing to. Another good opening is to be able to say that a press article or piece of news prompted you to write:

'I read in the *Pockwick Herald* last week that Pockwick Publicity Limited has just won the xyz contract, and wondered whether this means that the company will be in need of more fully-trained staff to handle the extra workload.'

'I was very interested to hear your radio interview yesterday on Radio Pockwick, and to learn that you are planning a third branch of Pockwick Accessories to open within the next two months.'

It is a good discipline to write speculative letters of application only to those employers you can greet with an opening something along these lines, and only to those employers whose name you know. Being able to do this means that you have good reason to believe they need you and could employ you if only they knew of your existence. Untargeted speculative applications or applications sent to personnel staff rather than managers with the power to hire, are a complete waste of time.

In a speculative application, your covering letter should express your versatility as a worker and pinpoint what you consider to be your own strengths. Follow the rules for covering letters. Do not name the position you would like but give the skills you can offer (you never know exactly what position could be on offer). At the end of your letter, ask for a meeting to discuss employment possibilities rather than ask for a job.

An example of a speculative letter of application is on page 122. There are a number of things to note about this example:

Dear Ms Smith

Your colleague Andrew Lawton suggested I contact you because
you are responsible for recruiting window-dressing personnel at
ABC Stores Ltd. I am a qualified window-dresser with seven
years' experience, and I am looking for a new challenge.

You will see from my enclosed CV that I have a record of
innovation and excellence, having won four national awards in the
past three years (photographs of the winning displays are also
enclosed). My experience is almost all in home furnishings and I
would welcome the opportunity to work with the market leaders in
this field, particularly as the company has such a strong reputation
for new and refreshing ideas.

I hope that we will be able to meet to discuss the possibility of my
joining your team. I will call you next week to arrange a mutually
convenient time.

Yours sincerely

- The writer has a contact and uses the connection right at the start of the letter to break the ice and to 'hook' the reader.
- There is a pithy description of the writer and a statement of the purpose of the letter in the first sentence.
- The writer is applying from a position of strength – her several awards make her an attractive prospect as an employee – and she is including photographs to back up her claim (see pages 138–9 for more on this).
- The crux of the application is that the writer is mirroring the employer's reputation for innovation with her own.
- The writer has taken the initiative away from the recipient (who might be interested in the applicant but may not get around to doing anything about it for weeks) by stating that she will call to arrange a meeting and by giving a deadline for this. Being organized, she has also made a note in her diary to remind herself to do this and filed a copy of her application with her research on the company so that she can find it easily when the time comes. She has also updated her contact records (see pages 37–40).
- A small amount of flattery goes a long way!

Telephone applications

Some job advertisements require that you telephone the advertisers to make an appointment for an interview. But beware! Advertisers often use this telephone call to screen out unwanted applicants right at the very start of the process. Therefore, prepare ahead of time for some questions. Have the advert and your CV in front of you when you call so that you have material to hand from which to take your cues. Have also a piece of paper and a pen poised to take notes of the company's location, the name of the person who will be interviewing you, and any details of the job you may be given.

Make the call as soon as you see the advertisement. Do not wait or you may find that the employer has made five appointments and has decided to make no more. If this happens you will probably hear those fatal words, 'Sorry, the job's gone.'

If you think you might clam up when speaking to the employer, write down your first line:

> 'I would like to speak to Mr Creswell please. Mr Creswell, my name is John Brown and I am calling in response to your advertisement for a barman in today's *Haynes Gazette*. I have bar experience and would like to be considered for the position. Would it be possible to arrange an interview?'

Here are some guidelines for good telephone conversations:

- Make sure that your environment is quiet so that you can hear clearly and can be heard.
- If you are using a public telephone box, take enough change with you: this could be a long conversation. Ideally, buy a pre-paid phonecard so that you are not bothered with the bleeping sound of money running out.
- Speak more slowly than you would usually, particularly if

you have an accent that may not readily be understood. Do not shout into the receiver.

- Be polite and patient. If your call 'gets lost' somewhere in the system, hang up and try again. Explain what has happened but try not to sound angry or critical. Receptionists and telephonists often pass comment on callers to the recipient before they put you through ('...it's a very rude woman calling about the job...'), and a single bad comment could cost you an interview.

- When taking down details of time and place, get into the habit of repeating the details back to the person you are speaking to. This acts as a check that you have everything down correctly and that there are no misunderstandings. If you do not know how to spell something (for example, the name of the person you will be meeting, or the street in which the company's offices are situated) ask for it to be spelled out. You will look about half as foolish doing this than when you turn up an hour late for your interview because you went to the wrong place.

- Have your diary to hand and double check that you can make the appointment being offered. On no account should you refuse an interview time because you are doing something that is leisure-related. If you are asked to suggest a time, ask for the earliest slot in the interview calendar. The interviewer will be fresher and may even spend more time with you if you are first. Never make an interview appointment and then call up to change it. With recruitment exercises that involve large numbers of people, the organizational problems to the recruiter are immense (particularly if a panel is involved). If you make these problems even greater by chopping and changing, you will not be very popular.

- Try to sound businesslike. If you think you have a problem with your telephone manner, listen to a telephonist or receptionist next time you are waiting in a foyer for an interview. You will hear how they are able to convey their messages while being economical with words, how they remain polite in the face of rudeness, how their voices are crystal clear.

- If planning a meeting, make sure that you have all the information you need (write yourself a checklist and put it by the phone if necessary): address, name of recruiter, address of company, date, day and time of interview.

- If you have made an appointment for an interview ask, if you think it appropriate, whether the recruiter has anything he can send by way of further information about the company and about the job you will be discussing. At the same time, volunteer to send a copy of your CV if appropriate. Advance information on both sides will make any meeting go more smoothly.

- If you know you have difficulty on the telephone, practice with your mentor. Do a few mock calls, and ask your mentor to make notes on tone, clarity, speed of talking, volume, how easy it was to understand what you were trying to say, the number of times you said 'ummm' or 'y'know'. Take the criticism in the spirit in which it is offered and remember your good qualities while working on the parts of the conversation you are not so good at.

If you make that telephone call and the person named in the advertisement is not there or unable to speak to you, do not leave a message. The onus is on you to get through and make the opportunity to state your case. Find out what time the recruiter will be available and make a note in your diary to call back at that time. This enables you to stay in control of when and under what conditions you have your first and most crucial conversation with the recruiter. Leave it to her and you never know what may be going on in your sitting room when she decides to return your call.

Troubleshooting

If you follow the advice given in this chapter you should be able to improve your contacts with prospective employers to the point that they will ask you to meet them. Advice on how to prepare for that event is given in the next chapter. If, however, this is not the case and your applications elicit a succession of negative responses, start trying to find out what you are doing wrong. Go back over your records. Could you be doing any of the following:

- Allowing your application to go out with spelling mistakes, crossings out, poor handwriting?
- Failing to match your skills, qualifications and experience to those required?
- Sending out your application too long after the advertisement has appeared?
- Failing to direct your application to a named person, or the right person?

- Failing to argue your case in a short covering letter?
- Failing to follow up speculative applications?
- Failing to make personal contact using your network?

Ask your mentor or partner to look at your applications. Can she see anything you may be doing badly? You may even need to change tack completely and target work that is in a different field before you start getting positive responses.

Whatever you do, keep at it, and treat your search for work as a serious 40-hour-a-week job. The whole process is a matter of honing your application skills until you find the employer who needs *you*.

INTERVIEWS AND MEETINGS

'Every time I make an appointment, I make a hundred men discontented and one ungrateful.'
Louis XIV of France (1638–1715)

Congratulations! You have received an invitation to attend an interview, or a first exploratory meeting with a possible employer. Either you contacted the employer in response to a situations vacant advertisement or your independent research or contacts told you that the employer was likely to be interested in taking on someone like you now or in the future. Whichever route you took to reach it, this meeting is your opportunity to let the employer know that he would benefit from your joining his team.

The pre-interview process, that of deselecting applicants on the basis of their CV and letter (or telephone call), was a negative process in which the selector said 'not him, not her, not her, not him...' Any interview or meeting is, by contrast, a positive event. However, it is also a complex interaction between two or more people. The purpose of an interview or meeting is to do one or more of the following things:

- To enable the employer to find out more about the candidate, and to assess suitability on the basis of: qualifications, experience, skills, motivation, demeanour, character.
- To enable you to find out what the job entails: location, environment, type of work, etc.

- To enable you to find out about the company's 'style' and 'culture': how its staff treat other people (i.e. you as an outsider) and how the company treats its staff.
- To show that the candidate can solve the employer's problems by becoming an employee or by selling your services to the employer as a contractor. (These two are, in fact, the same thing.)

It is helpful to consider the interview as an exchange of information rather than as an examination of you the candidate. The employer is trying to find out if you can give her what she needs, and wants to know what you would want in return.

While this meeting is just as important as any other, don't count your chickens before they are hatched. Even if you have received an invitation to an interview, do not give up your other work-search activities. Carry on scanning the situations vacant columns, continue following up contacts and don't stop searching high and low for other opportunities like this one. Consider this just another iron in the fire, and, if you or the employer decide that this is not the job for you, there will always be other avenues to explore.

Confirmation

The invitation to a meeting will probably suggest a date and time. Check your diary to make sure that you can attend. You may need to leave the whole day for final preparation and travel before the interview or for writing your interview report after the interview. Re-arrange your other appointments in order to be there. If there is absolutely no way you are going to make it (perhaps you have already confirmed another interview for the same day), call the company and ask to re-arrange it. If your invitation is written, your confirmation should be written (unless you are told to call instead). It is not essential to write this letter by hand, and it is probably better (especially if your handwriting is poor) to type it. Like the request for an application form (see page 115–6), your letter should be short and to the point

There is an example on page 132. Note that this letter includes all the details of the meeting (day, date, time and place) and include the name of any other person involved (you should be given this information in the invitation letter). This acts as a double-check both for you and for the interviewer.

Once you have confirmed that you can attend, you need to make room in your diary for interview preparation.

Preparation

The key to good interviews and meetings is preparation, and for your interview you will need to prepare on the following fronts:

- Information preparation: consolidating your research on the company and the job.
- Mental preparation: getting your ideas straight in your mind.
- Physical preparation: deciding what you will be wearing, what you will be taking with you and how you will get to the interview on time.

Dear Mr Jones,

      Thank you for your invitation to attend a meeting at your Greystone Street office at 10:30 a.m. on Monday 14th July 1997. This is to confirm that I will be able to attend.

      I look forward to meeting you and Mrs Howe on Monday.

            Yours sincerely

Information preparation

You should already have entries in your contact record and information in your file about the company and your contact with it. If the interview is the result of a speculative letter, you will probably already have much more information to hand than if you simply answered an advertisement. Read through what you have already gathered to refresh your memory on the reason and context of your contact.

If it was a speculative contact, what prompted you to get in touch? Who was the contact that suggested the name? What did you think the company might need that you could deliver?

If it was an advertisement of some sort, re-read the advert and any further information. Look through the copy of the application form or letter and CV that you sent them and work out why they may be interested in your application in particular.

Gather as much intelligence as you can about the job, the company and the interviewer. Find out too about how much people in the industry are being paid to do similar types of work at the same level as you. Start at the library, looking at:

- Business directories for factual information (size of company, location, number of branches, its activities, staff totals, profitability, turnover, etc.).
- Newspaper and magazine indexes to lead you to articles about the company for information on recent changes, contracts won, expansion, redundancies, etc.
- Job directories and books giving descriptions of the job to refresh your memory about what it normally entails.

Call the company's publicity or press department and ask for any written information they can send. Explain that you have an interview at the company, and that you are trying to find out more about it. Most press departments will be more than happy to help. When you find someone who has agreed to help you, take his name and remember to send him a thank-you note. Another contact made!

Your next option should be your network. Find an insider if you can: someone who has worked for the company and can give you plenty of personal insight into what to expect at the interview and what it might be like to join the company:

- Who is the person who will be interviewing you? Does she have the authority to hire you? What is she like? Does she have a reputation for being tough?
- What department would you be going into? How many people does it already employ? Is it seen as being on the leading edge of the company's activities or is it just jogging along?
- What is the inside story on the company itself? What kind of people does it usually employ (younger, older, men, women, etc.)? What does it value and reward in its staff?

If you cannot find anyone who has worked for the company in question, talk to people in the industry as a whole and ask what they know of the potential employer.

Finally in this part of your preparation, you will need to work out how much you want to be paid. While discussions of salary should always be kept until after you have been offered the job, it is advisable to be prepared with information in case events overtake you. You may be offered the job on the spot and there may be significant pressure to accept at once, or you may be asked to give a range from which negotiations would start if you were offered the job at a later date. Remember, however, that it is in your interest to postpone negotiations of salary until you are certain the employer has decided on you for the job.

The advertisement may give a salary range, but you should decide on a range for yourself in order to be ready to negotiate when the time comes. Work out what would be your minimum salary or wage: the amount you could comfortably survive on. Then try to find out what other people with your experience and doing similar jobs in the same industry are earning (a union official or Jobcentre staff may be able to help if you have no contacts who can give you the information you need). When you have fixed your minimum, work out the upper end of your scale: for an annual salary below about £25,000, say, £2,500 more. Then take a figure between these two and express your salary requirements as a range between the middle figure and the higher one. For example, you think you could survive on £14,500 per year, but would like to earn £17,000. Your salary range should be expressed as £15,500–£17,000. The employer will probably throw up his hands in horror at £17,000 but offer you £15,000, which is lower than your ideal, but still more than your minimum.

Mental preparation
After a few days researching the company in this way, you should have a pretty clear idea of the animal you are going to

be tackling! Now it is time to start asking yourself those questions again, but this time, you are trying to put yourself into the interviewer's shoes. Try to work out what she wants of you and decide how you are going to show her that you can supply her needs.

It is helpful at this stage to make notes, perhaps by jotting down your answers to the following questions:

- What are the qualifications the employer thinks you need to do the job? List them with the grade and date. If you think the employer might ask for qualifications you don't have, could you argue that your long experience means the same as the raw qualification? Be prepared to make this point in the interview.

- What is the experience the employer thinks you need to do the job? Write it down and then give a list of your experience that matches. If you don't have all the right experience, write down other comparable experience (you may have done this if you wrote a covering letter, see page 110). Be prepared to discuss matching experience and to point out similar experience at the interview.

- What are the skills the employer thinks you need to do the job? List them. List evidence to show that you have these skills. If you don't have some of the skills required, could you acquire them? Or do you have comparable skills? Again, be prepared to discuss your matching skills and to argue that the skills you do not have could be acquired or could be substituted with other skills you have.

- What kind of person do you think you need to be to do the job well (temperament, ability to work with others, to work alone or unsupervised, etc). List examples to show that you are this kind of person.
- How does the job match your requirements in terms of location, environment, remuneration, training and prospects?
- Think yourself into the shoes of an employee doing the job. What do you think would be important qualities, from the point of view of the employer, and, perhaps from the point of view of the customer?

You will see that most of these questions are directly related to the form used to analyse an advertisement. However, this time you should be concentrating on amassing evidence to show that you fit the employer's idea of what the job entails. It is important first to imagine what the employer is trying to find in the ideal candidate, using the job advertisement and your knowledge of the work, and second to prove that, one way or another, your profile has all the right characteristics.

While you are doing this, also note down any questions you would like to ask the interviewer. There is often time towards the end of an interview for you to ask questions of your own, and it shows assertiveness and initiative if you have some to ask (see page 163–5).

Practice your testimony

A vital stage in your mental preparation is to practice articulating your evidence. Stand in front of a mirror and talk to yourself about your experience, your qualifications, your skills. Look for the right words, dynamic words, positive words, to describe your profile. Smile at yourself and make eye contact with your reflection as you speak. Later in this chapter is a list of the questions you may encounter in an interview. Practice answering these in particular. Avoid parroting off stock answers, however. Try to say it a slightly different way each time you practice.

With a little practice each day over the week leading up to the interview you will find that your confidence will start to build. You may even start to look forward to the meeting.

More information on how to plan and execute speaking events (for an interview is no less than a speaking engagement), is given in Collins Pocket Reference Public Speaking, which will also give you some techniques to calm your nerves.

Hard evidence

Is there anything you could take to your interview that would prove to the interviewer something about your abilities and past experiences? In some industries it is the norm to show a portfolio of recent work, but if you are not an artist, illustrator, photographer, designer or writer, what could you show? Perhaps you compiled a report – take a copy (make sure that the information is not confidential). Have you been the subject of a magazine article? Take a copy with you. Do you make unusual things? Take one with you. Model your own jewellery, wear clothes you have made (if they are appropriate to the occasion), take photographs of interiors you have decorated.

Have you won an award? Leave the trophy at home! Do you have a testimonial (an open letter of reference)? Take it with you. It's all a matter of choosing which article would be the most powerful evidence, and which is the most relevant.

If you do decide to take hard evidence with you, check it for presentability. You may find that your child has dismantled your portfolio or that it needs to be rearranged to highlight certain items relevant to the job. You may need to make fresh copies of clippings or photographs.

Practical preparation

A few days before the meeting, decide what you are going to wear. It is best to be formal. Men should choose a conservative suit and tie or at least a jacket and trousers, and women should go for a suit or skirt or trousers and jacket. Don't take the risk of wearing jeans and a T-shirt. Even if a company is informal about its dress code, the risk of appearing too casual is just too great. Just this once, err on the side of formality. However, there is an exception to every rule. You may be in the fashion industry, for instance, and want to show that you have a sense of current youth-culture style. In which case, the conservative suit and tie will be a liability rather than an asset.

Avoid wearing a great deal of jewellery, even if you always do. It will distract the interviewer's attention from what you are trying to say. Keep make-up subtle and avoid bright nail polish. Don't be tempted to wear heels that may give you trouble walking. If you buy new shoes, break them in before the interview – bleeding blisters are not a pretty sight and the pain will ruin your concentration.

Make sure that the overall effect is of good grooming. If you need to have your hair cut, do it a few days before the interview – everyone recognizes that just-cut look. Shave, twice if you have to in order to achieve a clean finish, or clip your beard so that it is neat. People with longer hair should ensure that it does not obscure their face – you will need to make good eye contact with the interviewer, and it will irritate her if she cannot see the expression on your face.

If you haven't worn your outfit for a while, try it on a few days in advance and check it thoroughly for moth holes, missing buttons, cleanliness, frayed edges, worn shoe laces, broken down heels. Check that your watch works. If you do find anything that needs to be attended to, you still have time to do it.

At this point you should also put some thought into what you are going to carry with you. It is always a good idea to take something to hold (it gives you something to do with your hands and stops you putting them in your pockets, which looks too relaxed). Try to keep it neat and simple: a slim briefcase or an acetate folder containing your paperwork, or a plain handbag. Avoid carrying armloads of shopping or bulky objects with you. If you are nervous, you are bound to fall over them, and there may not be space to put them neatly out of the way. Make sure that any accessories you take are in just as good order as your clothing. Many well-turned out people are let down by a battered brief-case or worn out handbag. Strive above all for a no-fuss, orderly appearance.

Travel plans

At this time you should also be thinking about the travel

arrangements you will need to make to get to the interview with as few problems as possible. A well-planned journey will ensure you are in the right place at the right time and in the right frame of mind.

If you have never been to the place where the interview is due to be held, it is worthwhile doing a dry run if at all possible. Start by estimating how long it will take you to get there and planning your journey. It is best to go at the same time of day as for the real thing, so that you have an accurate picture of traffic conditions.

This need not be a wasted journey. While you are at the company's location, have a look around at the buildings and familiarize yourself with the feel of it all. After all, fear is usually fear of the unknown, and so the more familiar you are with the people and place, the less nervous you will feel on the day. Perhaps ask at reception if there is any company information available that you can take home. If you have done your pre-interview research properly, you should have everything the company usually provides, but this excuse gets you inside the building a little way. Explain that you have an interview and would like to do some last-minute reading. (If you are offered a copy of a report that you already have, accept it with good grace and thanks – don't turn it down). If a receptionist helps you in this way, don't forget to note down his or her name and send a thank-you note straight away. Yet another contact made!

Last minute preparation
Plan to get a good night's sleep the night before your interview. Steer clear of alcohol if you can, and eat early in the evening –

you will sleep better for this. A warm bath is a good idea, and reading a book or magazine is more relaxing than watching television. Don't be tempted to do any last-minute cramming. If you have worked on your research in the past few days or weeks in the way suggested, you should be perfectly well-prepared. Lay out your clothes for the following day and double-check them carefully. Gather together anything else you might like to take with you. Here are some ideas:

- the advert for the job
- copy of your CV
- travel tickets
- notebook
- purse or wallet
- umbrella
- pain killers
- spectacles case/cleaner
- pocket sewing kit
- handkerchief
- copy of your application form
- portfolio or other 'evidence'
- something to read
- pen
- spare stockings or tights
- necessary medication
- spare shoe laces
- contact lens eyedrops
- sanitary supplies
- watch
- a note of the interviewer's name and telephone number

Handling pre-interview nerves

You may be the kind of person who takes all this in their stride, never experiencing more than a moment's anxiety. However, if you are anything like the rest of us, it is only natural that you will experience some pre-interview nerves. If you've got it bad, you may not be able to sleep the night before, or you may become forgetful or irritable. Here are some notes to remember that might help you reduce the stress of the interview:

- Confidence comes from preparation. If you have prepared thoroughly, you should know where you are going and what you are going to say when you get there.
- Eat properly the night before the interview and during the day. Poor nutrition can have a profound effect on your anxiety level – keeping vitamin intake at correct levels can also help. (However, avoid strong, spicy foods or garlic, which may be distasteful for the interviewer.)
- Keep the event in perspective. This interview would be terrifyingly important if it were your last or only chance. But this is not your last or only chance. If you have followed the advice so far, you will have plenty of other options to consider, so that if this avenue turns into a dead end you have others to explore. If it is not quite so important as you thought, why are you so nervous?
- If you have found out as much as you can about the company, the job and the interview itself, you should know what reasonably to expect. If you know what is coming, you should not be anxious.
- The people you are going to see do not have the power of life and death over you. There is no need to be frightened of them. They are just ordinary people doing their jobs.
- If you are really nervous, imagine what is the worst thing that can happen to you? The worst thing you can think of, apart from failing to get the job (and we have already dealt with that), is being laughed out of the room. Well, you wouldn't want to work for such rude people, would you? So in this case, you could simply get up and leave. What is there to worry about in that? Try to imagine other

worst-case-scenarios, and then rationalize them. There is always a way to cope when the 'worst' happens, so why worry.

- Practice deep, slow breathing to combat that fluttering in your stomach and to steady your voice. Its amazing how three deep breaths can clear your head and bring you back to sanity.

If you are the kind of person who becomes nervous easily, you might consider taking up a relaxation technique that could help to control nerves in the long-term. Yoga classes will help you learn to calm down and relax. Voice training, the Alexander technique and acting training also include exercises for relaxation and physical control. Your local adult education centre probably runs classes.

Arrival

Aim to arrive at the interview location about 15 minutes early. You will need to wait for your turn, but it is better than being late. Try not to smoke once inside the building itself, and check your appearance before you go through the door. You are on view to everyone in the company from that moment on, so don't let yourself down for a moment.

Introduce yourself at reception, saying that you have an interview. Give the time and the name of the person you are meeting. In a well-run company, the receptionist should be expecting you. If you popped in the day before on your dry run (see page 143), he or she may even recognize you.

Have something to read while you are waiting, or use the

time to talk to the reception staff (without being a pest, of course). Most reception areas have brochures and reports relating to the company, but you should also have something with you to read. Today's newspaper, a trade magazine or a book would be ideal.

While you are waiting you should also be taking in everything you can about the company, making mental notes on your first impressions. Does it seem efficient and well-organized? Is the foyer large and luxurious or cramped and grubby? Are you being treated with courtesy or dismissed with a smirk? Is the place busy or quiet?

Do not spend time gazing at other candidates, imagining how much better they must be than you are. Do not speculate on how their chances of getting the job are compared to yours. This will simply make you more nervous and less confident. You are there with the rest because, on paper, you are as good as the rest.

If the company is interviewing a large number of people and your interview is late on in the day, you may find that the process is running behind schedule. Be patient, and don't take your irritation out on anyone else. In a company where courtesy is valued, you will already have an apology, and will be kept informed of what is happening. However, it is unreasonable to be kept waiting for too long. After about half an hour beyond your interview time, you should find out how much longer you can expect to be kept waiting. If you feel you are being treated without respect, ask to make an appointment for another day. Of course, you run the risk of losing the opportunity to interview altogether, but perhaps the incident shows that the company is inefficient and that its staff treat outsiders badly. Do you really want to work for them?

Interview formats

An interview can take one of several forms:

- The informal meeting in which you are ostensibly 'finding out' about the company.
- The informal one-to-one interview to which you have been invited to discuss a particular vacancy.
- Formal interviews in which there is more than one interviewer.
- Group interviews, residential courses and tests.
- The 'business meeting' in which you are telling the company about your activities and finding out if the company can make use of your services.

You will probably already have a good idea into which category your interview falls from your letter of invitation, but if you have not been told what format your interview will take, it may be worthwhile finding out, so that you know what to expect.

Fact-finding meetings

In an informal fact-finding meeting, you will probably be talking to one person about the company and possible openings for people with your skills as part of your research (see pages 51–2). The meeting will probably be very short, but you should treat it in the same way as any other interview: any exposure to a person who has the power to employ you is important.

One-to-one interviews

Interviews with just one person can either be formal in style or very informal, particularly in a small company. If the company is only one or two people strong, expect to be interrupted by telephone calls and other events. Try not to get annoyed, but to treat this interview as seriously as any other. Do not be lulled into a false sense of security by informality. Stay polite and attentive. Don't let your guard down so that you lose consciousness of yourself and start to talk without thinking. Weigh your words and make each one count. The game is still the same.

Interviews with two or more people

You may find that when you enter the interview room, you are faced with two or even more people (panels of perhaps as many as six or eight interviewers are not unknown, particularly for jobs in the public sector).

If there are two interviewers, one is probably the personnel manager and the other is the manager for whom you would be working if you got the job. The personnel manager is likely to ask questions relating to facts (your qualifications, for example), while the department manager will be more interested in talking about the skills you could bring to the position.

Panel interviews are probably the most nerve-wracking of all. However, you should have advance warning and your preparation will carry you a long way.

Group interviews and residential courses

Some interviewers like to interview candidates in groups. This kind of selection is often carried out by large firms at the second interview stage. The purpose is to find out more about the behaviour of each of the candidates.

The interview may take the form of a group discussion. If this is the case, don't dominate the floor with your opinions, and don't get angry or dismissive if people offer opposing views. Make your point clearly and then shut up and allow someone else to have their say. If you cannot think of anything new to add to the discussion, simply say that you agree with so-and-so and repeat her point. Ask people for agreement when you have made your point: 'I would say that this is the answer, don't you agree?'

In some group interviews, the candidates are asked to take part in some kind of activity. These exercises are usually to test cooperation and leadership qualities. Remember that cooperation is just as important as leadership, so don't be tempted to be dictatorial.

You may even be asked to attend a residential course which involves many activities. Remember in these cases that you will be under scrutiny most of the time. You can relax, but don't get drunk in the hotel bar in the evenings, and try to appear alert and interested at all times.

Tests

Many employers use tests of some kind to find out more about candidates. Some tests work better than others. For example, psychometric tests, in which the candidate responds to a long list of questions on attitudes and behaviour, have been largely discredited as having a serious cultural bias. Others rely for their accuracy in their description of your character type on the person who is analysing the results of the test.

In some industries, candidates are always tested for skills: secretarial work is a good example, in which candidates may take a typing and shorthand test. In these cases candidates will be perfectly used to the test.

Your invitation to interview should say whether you should be prepared to be tested and tell you what form the test will take. Make sure that you revise or practice as appropriate and follow the usual rules for examinations and other tests. Here are some notes:

- Read the instructions, or listen carefully to the person telling you what to do. If you are confused, ask. If told to do so, read the test through from start to finish before you begin.
- If you are stuck on one question, go on to the next. You may have time at the end to go back.
- If you have finished before your time is up, don't stand up and walk away, but go back and check your answers.

The 'business meeting'

This type of interview is very different from the others. There is no job on offer. Instead, you are making work for yourself, either by moving into a new area of the company you already work for, thus dodging redundancy, or by aquiring new clients for your freelance or consultancy activities.

Your agenda at this meeting is to argue that the company has a 'problem' that you can solve, a need that you can fulfil. At this interview, therefore, the onus is on you to lead the discussion. This should naturally lead to questions and answers as the meeting progresses.

It is probably wise to start with a formal introduction of yourself and an elaboration of the reasons for wanting to meet.

> 'As you know I have worked for 15 years as manager of xyz department. In recent years it has become increasingly obvious that efficiency has been damaged through old operating systems, and I would like to discuss a solution with you today.'

Give your credentials at the start. State your aims clearly to show that there is a definite reason for the meeting, and that you expect a certain outcome.

Next, you will need to outline your argument: describing the areas in which you feel you can be of service, and enumerating the reasons why you (and no other) are the person to help. You may like to send your contact this information in advance: an outline of your argument with as much back-up evidence as you can muster, so that time is not spent going over the details. This document could also act as a prompt for you or for your contact's questions as you put your case.

Your aim in discussing your proposal is to get agreement that your analysis is correct. Present the information and expect questions relating to it so that the conversation gradually comes round to this point and you can then go on to describing how you would act on this analysis. Make out a clear action plan:

'It seems to me that the system would take about two weeks to install (but this need not disrupt day-to-day work). Staff training could take place on two consecutive afternoons immediately after installation, followed by refreshers and advanced training of one day at two-monthly intervals.'

In circumstances like this, your contact is going to want to know how much he is going to be asked to pay. As with any other interview, be prepared to give a range, but avoid in-depth discussions of money until your contact has returned to you with a positive response. At that stage you are in a much better position to negotiate a good fee.

At the end of the meeting, your contact will probably indicate that he wants time to discuss with colleagues and to consider. Try to find out when you might get an answer and make it clear that if there are further questions, you would welcome them. Follow-up your meeting with a polite phone call a few days later. (See pages 72–4 for more advice on making work for yourself.)

General tips for interviews

- In all social situations, people make up their minds very quickly about other people. As soon as they lay eyes on them, they are looking for ways to categorize them, to sum them up as friend or foe. This is why first impressions are so important. As you stand up to shake hands, or enter the room for the first time, be fully aware of making the best possible impression in the first few moments.

- At the start of the interview, find a comfortable and upright seated posture, sitting well back in the chair and not on the edge of it. Don't slouch or hang your head. Don't sprawl if you have been given space (perhaps on a sofa) to do so. Cross your legs and fold you hands in your lap. Don't cross your arms: this is a very strong defensive signal that the interviewer is likely to recognize. Avoid scratching, tapping your feet, twirling your spectacles, tilting the chair backwards, expansive hand gestures or any other irritating habit. If you don't think you do any of these things, ask your partner – and don't be insulted when he or she tells you a few home truths. Don't put your briefcase or handbag on the interviewer's desk. Place it on the floor to the side of you, but make sure no-one is going to trip over it.

- Be aware that you are communicating not only through spoken words, but also through body-language. Make eye contact with the interviewer; smile; nod to express agreement or enthusiasm; vary the tone of your voice so that it is more expressive, use your hands to amplify what you are saying (but avoid waving them around too much).

- If you are being interviewed by more than one person, make sure that you can see all the interviewers by a simple turn of the head. If you cannot do this, move your chair so that you can before the interview starts. If the interviewer is sitting in front of a bright light (a window, perhaps), so that you cannot see his face, or so that you are blinded, move so that the effect is less problematic, or politely ask the interviewer to draw a blind. Make sure that your chair is in the right position and then do not move it again until the end of the interview.

- Look at the interviewer when you are being asked a question. Make eye contact. This is very important – people who do not make eye contact are considered shifty. However, it often embarrasses people if you hold their gaze for too long, so break the contact before this happens.

- In a panel interview, look at the person who is asking the question, and direct your answer to her. When you have finished your answer look slowly along the line of faces to show that you are ready for the next question.

- Before you answer a question, pause for a moment. This will give you time to collect your thoughts and you will be considered to be a thoughtful person. Speaking before you have formulated your answer in your head could be disastrous.

- In panel interviews it is likely that the subject of conversation moves back and forth, from one subject to another and back to the first. This is not because the interviewers are trying to confuse you, but because they want to follow up your answers to previous questions. It's up to you to keep the pace of the interview manageable. Pausing before you speak helps.

- Do not smoke in interviews, even if you are offered a cigarette and the interviewer is smoking.

- Do not accept offers of hot drinks or alcohol. Hot drinks are invariably too hot to drink quickly between answers and alcohol can have a surprising effect when you are tense and nervous. In the worst case, you may drop the cup or burn your mouth. If a drink is offered, water will help keep your mouth moist and doesn't do too much damage if sent sprawling across the interviewer's desk!

- Never swear in an interview, even if the interviewer does.
- Don't talk too little or too much. An interview full of monosyllabic answers will get you nowhere (but there are moments when plain 'yes' or 'no' is perfectly suitable, see page 159). When appropriate, elaborate your answer with one or two pieces of evidence, but avoid anecdotes. Some interviewers have the nasty habit of waiting after you have finished speaking to see if, embarrassed by the silence, you will continue. If you do it is likely that you will have nothing considered to say, you may even start to talk nonsense or to contradict what you just said. Don't. If you have given an answer and backed it up with a piece of hard evidence, leave it at that. If you feel embarrassed by a longer than normal silence, simply say that you have nothing more to say on that point and wait expectantly for the next question. This should show the interviewer that you are not going to be tricked into being foolish.
- In general, speak for a little more than half the time in an interview. While it is impossible to time each of your answers and calculate how much more air-time you have left to complete your 50%. Simply balance your speaking time with that of the interviewer. Try to keep your individual answers to below two minutes. The ability to listen carefully to what is being said is just as valuable as being able to articulate your thoughts, so make sure that

you show you are a listener as well.

- Do not be distracted if the interviewer takes notes while you are speaking. There is nothing sinister in this. He simply wants to be able to remember the salient points of your argument.

- Never, ever be tempted to criticize your previous employers or colleagues, even if the interviewer expresses a negative opinion. This shows you have a capacity for disloyalty and gossip, something no-one wants to think they have in their staff. However, don't lie about what are manifestly poor working relationships or serious incidents. Keep your explanations on a profes-sional level. Try to spot awkward questions like this in advance, and rehearse your responses carefully.

The interview process

Most interviews follow a certain pattern. The more interviews you attend the more easily you will recognize the pattern as it emerges. Of course, this does depend on the interviewer being experienced. Inexperienced interviewers often do things differently. The normal pattern, however, is as follows:

- Greetings and introduction, during which you will probably shake hands with the interviewer(s). Then you will normally be asked to sit down, and you should make yourself comfortable as quickly as possible. See page 152.
- Breaking the ice. As you settle down, the interviewer will probably ask you about your journey or talk about the weather: any small talk to break the ice and give you time

to settle down. Don't be tempted to give a blow-by-blow account of your journey, but you could say that you popped over the day before to pick up a brochure from the press office and so knew where you were going.

- Checking the facts. To move into the question-and-answer routine, the interviewer will probably check with you some of the facts mentioned in your CV or application. Some of these questions may appear obvious to you ('so you are applying to be head chef?'), but answer them politely with a simply 'yes' or 'that's correct'.
- Principal question-and-answer session aimed at finding out whether the interviewee is capable of doing the job; has the requisite experience, qualifications and skills; is the kind of person who will fit in to the company; and has the correct motivations (i.e. will she stay in the job long enough, or does she have the drive to see the project through to completion?). This is the core of the interview.
- Questions from the interviewee.
- Closing. You will be told what happens next and when to expect a decision. Thanks will be offered for your attendance (and you should thank the interviewer for her interest). After more hand-shaking the interviewee is seen out.

Interview questions analysed

The purpose of an interview is to find out whether the candidate and the employer can match their needs. It often seems that the decision-making is all on the interviewer's side, but you should try to see this as an exchange of information rather than an examination.

There are two types of interview question, and if you realise which kind a particular question is, you can frame your answer in the most appropriate way. 'Closed questions' require a simple 'yes', 'no', or a factual answer:

Q: How old are you?
A: Twenty-five.
Q: You went to school at Littlewick Grammar?
A: That's correct.

'Open questions' require that you answer the question and then elaborate:

Q: Why do you think you would be a good candidate for this position?
A: It seems to me that the job requires x, y and z skills and these I learned and consolidated in my last two positions at ABC Ltd and UVW Ltd.
Q: Are there any other qualities a good lion tamer should have?
A: Yes. He should be disciplined and enjoy maintaining a routine. In my experience, the lions become unsettled when their routine is upset and that could lead to all sorts of problems.
Q: Why should we employ you?
A: Because I am well-qualified on paper and I have ten

years' experience doing a similar job. What's more, I am constantly working on ways to improve the workings of the department. For instance I installed an xyz machine when I was at Davies and Sons, and this cut absenteeism in half. You will be getting an innovator as well as a manager.

At the same time as open and closed questions there are also many different angles from which the interviewer could ask questions. However, underneath, the real questions to be answered are very simple:

- Can you do the job (skills, qualifications, experience)?
- Why do you want the job (are your loyalties with the employer or do you have more important things to think about, are you going to leave after a short time)?
- What are your strengths and weaknesses?
- Would you fit into the company? Are you 'our kind of person'? Would you do things the way we do them?
- What are your behaviour patterns? Are you disruptive, adventurous, quiet, patient? Would you shout at a customer if you were in a bad mood?

Your research and practice has all been geared towards training you to answer just these kinds of questions. You should know where your strengths are and be able to give evidence for each assertion. You should know something of what the job entails and therefore what the employer expects to hear on that front. If you have done your research, you should know the kinds of people the company employs and how it encourages them to behave. The skill is to be able to decipher what the interviewer is really asking you and to respond sensibly.

Here are some examples of questions you might be asked at an interview. In your preparation, you might find it useful to go through this list and write down your answer, keeping in mind the specific position you are interviewing for.

- Tell me about yourself.
- What in particular do you feel you have to offer this company?
- Why do you want to/why did you leave your present job?
- Tell me what you know about this company.
- What do you know about the job on offer?
- Where did you hear about this job?
- What made you apply for this particular job?
- What do you consider your strengths to be?
- What do you consider your weaknesses to be?
- What would you like to be doing in five years time?
- Do you feel you are suitably qualified for this position?
- Don't you think that you might be over-qualified for this post?
- Are you applying for other jobs at the moment?
- How have you used your time while you have been unemployed?
- You seem to have had a number of jobs in a very short space of time. Why is that?
- You seem to have stayed in your last job for a long time.

Why was that?

- How do you cope with stress?
- What do you think your most important personal qualities are?
- Tell me about your career to date.
- How do you feel about working with the general public?
- How would you sum up this company's public image?
- Do you feel that this job will be demanding enough for you?
- Who put together your CV for you?
- Why do you think you have not found a job yet?
- Why did you choose the subjects you studied at school/college?
- What did you enjoy about your college life?
- What was your favourite subject at school/college?
- What was your least favourite subject?
- Do you think you did yourself justice in your exams?
- Why did you not continue in education?
- How did you manage to work full-time and study for a degree at the same time?
- How do you think your last boss would describe you?
- How did you get on with your colleagues in your last job?
- What problems did you encounter in your last job and how did you overcome them?
- If you got this job, how long do you think you would stay with us?
- What do you think are the most important qualities for the person taking up this position?
- What skills and experiences would you be able to bring us

that would benefit us as a company?

- What did you learn in your last job that has prepared you for this one?
- Do you consider yourself to be a good team-member? Or do you prefer to work alone?
- What are the recent developments that have changed your field of work over the past few years?
- How do you keep up with changes in your field of work?
- Why were you selected for redundancy?
- You lack xyz experience. How do you think you will make up for that?
- Would you be prepared to study in the evenings?
- Do you think you might be a little old/young for the job?
- Is there any part of the job on offer that you have not done before, or feel worried about?
- All of your colleagues will be of the opposite sex. How do you feel about being the only man/woman on the team?
- Do you have family or friends in this industry?
- What improvements would you have made in your last job?
- What qualities do you think are most important in a manager?
- How would you describe your management style?
- Do you consider yourself aggressive/passive?
- What do you think is the most effective means of motivating people?
- How do you manage your time?
- What was your worst mistake/biggest failure?
- What was your greatest success?

- Why did you embark upon a career in this field?
- Are you still happy to be in this field?
- Do you think your career has developed in line with your career plans, or not?
- How would taking this job would fit in with your career plan?
- How important is money to you?
- When did you last take a holiday, and where did you go?
- How many hours do you work in an average week?
- Do you think you command respect among colleagues?
- Do you socialize with work colleagues?
- Do you often work weekends?
- How would you define success?
- Do you hold positions of responsibility outside work?
- How do you spend your time outside work?
- Tell me about: the last book you read/the last film you saw/the last play you saw (any leisure item from the CV).
- Are you politically active?
- Would you accept this job if we offered it to you?
- Tell me why you think I should hire you?

Once in a while, your concentration may lapse and you could find the interviewer staring at you, waiting for an answer to the question you have not heard. If this happens, simply admit you were distracted and ask politely that she repeat the question. If you do not understand a question that is put to you, say that you do not understand, and ask for the question to be repeated. In an extreme situation you may find that you cannot recall a good example of your using a skill that is under discussion.

Once again, admit what has happened: 'I'm sorry, my mind has gone blank. Could we come back to that question later?' No-one will blame you for this, and often, you will gain marks for handling the situation so well.

Questions of remuneration

Many interviewers will try to find out how much you are earning now or how much you think you are worth. Try to avoid answering this question at this time. You will be in a much stronger position to bargain when the employer has decided that he definitely wants you and no other to do the job. Say politely that you think questions of money are a little premature, but that you would be happy to discuss them when you have a firm job description and indication of the whole package. If you are pressed, give a range, rather than a single figure, saying that the actual sum would depend on the job itself and any other forms of remuneration (company car, health care, etc.) on offer.

You should have given some thought to this in advance (see pages 134–5) and have with you a note of the amount you want to earn and the minimum you will accept. At this stage the recruiter will probably just make a note for future reference (see page 172–4).

Candidates' questions

Towards the end of an interview, you will probably be asked if you have any questions you want to ask the interviewer. Have some thought out in advance. If you think your mind is likely to go blank in the stress of the interview, write them down, and don't be embarrassed to take out your notes. Far from making you seem foolish, this simply indicates that you take the interview seriously enough to have done some thinking.

Don't ask about holiday entitlement and pay rises. In the first place, discussions on these fronts are part of the negotiation of the actual employment package and should take place after you have been offered the post (see page 172–6). Secondly, putting emphasis on rewards in this way make you seem grasping and uninterested in doing the job for its own sake.

You may like to ask about the mechanism for promotion and assessments, for example, or about a recent event that you have learned about in the press:

> 'I read in the Hosiers Times that the opening up of the former Soviet Union has meant new opportunities for British hosiers. Is the company planning to take advantage of this?'

Or you may like to ask more questions about the job:

> 'In the advertisement you said earlier that there may be some travel involved in the job. When do you expect this to take place and how often would the necessity arise?'

You may be able to pick up on information given in the interview itself. Note down points you would like to return to and refer to them when you are invited to ask questions. If you did have questions, but the answers were covered in the interview, say so:

'I did have a couple of questions, but I think they have been adequately covered by the information you have given me. Thank you.'

If you have brought something to show the interviewer and have not already been invited to do so, politely offer to show it at this point.

Don't ask too many questions. At this stage, the interviewer is probably hoping to get a cup of coffee before the next candidate arrives, or is already running late. Don't rush through your questions, but on the other hand don't keep the interviewer in reluctant conversation for the next half-hour.

You could also use this time to add any information that you feel you have not been given the opportunity to bring out in the interview. Do not go over ground already covered, but make sure that you mention things you feel the interviewer needs to know to make a decision.

You walk out into the street and pause for a moment to reflect. Was your experience of the last half-hour good or bad? Do you feel relieved it is over, or are you excited at the opportunity that seems to have been laid at your feet? Whatever happened 'in there' you have much more to do now than just waiting for a decision.

POST-INTERVIEW ACTIVITIES

'A verbal contract isn't worth the paper it's written on.'
Samuel Goldwyn (1884–1974)

After you have been through the rigours of an interview, it is tempting to sit back and do nothing until the decision comes through. There is nothing wrong with taking the rest of the afternoon off, or rewarding yourself in some other way. You really have earned it! But very soon, you need to go back to the routine of research and application. While you are continuing with your normal work-search activities, you will also need to do some follow-up work.

The very first thing to do, though, is to write a thank-you note to the person who conducted your interview. Obviously, if you were interviewed by a panel of 12, you cannot write 12 notes. Direct your thanks principally to the person who organized the interview, and ask her to convey your gratitude to the other interviewers. In thinking about the interview, some things may occur to you that, had you mentioned them, might have strengthened your case. This is your opportunity to add them. See page 167 for an example.

Debriefing

The next most important thing to do is to debrief yourself. It is important to think through your performance and recall the questions put to you and the answers you gave. Assess your

Dear Miss James

Thank you for taking the time to meet with me yesterday with regard to your vacancy for a studio manager. It was interesting to learn more about the position, and I would like to repeat my eagerness to be considered.

You asked during the interview whether I had any experience of handling budgets and I mentioned the job in which I monitored budgets in the absence of my senior. However, I now recall that when I was active in our Student's Union I was for a time responsible for monitoring the budget and ensuring that the accountants received all the information they required. I would then report to members of the committee. I therefore believe I have quite significant experience of accounting procedures and could quickly learn your particular system.

Thank you once again for your attention. I will hope to hear from you in the next few days.

Yours sincerely

own performance. Do you think you did yourself justice? Do you feel you were given enough opportunities to explain yourself fully? Which questions did you stumble on? Make a note to work on your answers so that you are better able to cope if the same or similar questions arise in a future interview. It might be useful to make out a report for your files using the form on pages 170–1 as a guideline.

If you were sent to an interview by an employment agent or recruitment consultant, send him a thank-you note as well. Call him the next day to discuss the interview. He may already have had some feedback on your performance from the interviewer and may be able to give you some advice or information that could give you a better chance next time.

Use all of this information to analyse and improve your interview performance. Some of us are just naturally good at meeting new people and have the confidence to articulate answers clearly. Most of us, however, suffer from nerves and are often less than relaxed when meeting strangers. Spotting your weaknesses is the first step towards remedying them and all you need is practice.

Chasing a response

At the end of the interview, a polite and organized interviewer would have told you when you can expect to have a decision. If the date passes and you have no response, leave it a couple more days – your letter may have been held up in the post or the interviewer may have been away from work for some reason. After this you should make a polite telephone call to the interviewer explaining who you are and that you had expected to receive word before now. There is probably a very good reason why the response has not come.

Dealing with No

For every candidate offered work there are a number of others who are not offered work. If the company interviews a shortlist of five for a single vacancy. It stands to reason that four of those people have to be turned down. This is a fact of life.

If one of those turned down is you, it is always a blow. You may feel rejected, worthless and angry. You may think you have wasted your time. You put in all that work and got nowhere. You have the right to think this way for about half an hour. Then it is time to put back on your positive attitude. You have it in your power to persuade somebody to offer you work. You got through to the interview stage once, so why shouldn't you do it again? And with every interview you have under your belt you become more expert at answering the questions and putting your case.

After each 'No' response, write a letter back, saying that you hope your application will be kept on file. If they could not offer you this job, perhaps another will come along in a couple of months, or perhaps the person who got the job was not so suitable after all and resigned after only a short time. There is another opportunity. Make a note in your diary to make a telephone call one month from now to check out the possibilities.

Make up your mind to keep on working at all your other work-search activities. Change your angle slightly. Work out what is strong and what is weak about your applications and about your interview performance. Be prepared to change tack

Interview Report

Company name _____

Date of interview _____

Job title _____

Name of principal interviewers _____

Position _____

Interview style (formal? panel? informal?) _____

Length of interview _____

Number of other candidates _____

Test? _____

Best question/answer _____

_____

_____

_____

_____

_____

Worst question/answer _____

_____

_____

Personal performance

_____

_____

marks out of ten

Extra information about the job

_____

_____

_____

Impressions of the company

_____

_____

completely if you think that you really have come up against a brick wall. Identify what skills and experience you are lacking. Consider extra training, other unpaid work activities, part-time work, anything you can add to your CV and talk about at interviews. Consider whether your expectations may be unrealistic and if you have to, take advice on this. Don't stop until you have what you want.

Handling an offer

Of course, unless something has gone disastrously wrong on the interviewer's side, one person in that group of five is going to be offered the job, and sooner or later that person is going to be you. The interviewer may even make up her mind on the spot and offer you the job before the interview has finished! If this is the case, be enthusiastic, but do not commit yourself to a firm acceptance until all the negotiations have taken place. At this stage all you need to say is that you would be happy to accept, subject to negotiation of the details of salary, working hours, etc. (See pages 134–5 on negotiating pay.)

The employer will normally make you a written offer, which should include details of the entire package, including:

- rate of pay and when you can expect to be paid (monthly, weekly)
- hours and place of work
- holiday entitlement and rules relating to sickness benefit
- pension and health insurance details (if any)
- any other benefits (free lunches, luncheon vouchers, company car, etc)

- a description of the job, including job title, responsibilities, targets, etc.
- Details of any commission or bonus system that may be in operation
- Details of any probationary period
- The system of salary increases and promotions

At this stage, sit down and take a long, hard look at the whole package. Go back to the notes on your personal needs, and see how this package fits in with what you said you wanted in return for your skills. Is there anything in the package that you would really hate (is the company so far away that you would have to commute for long periods each day, for example?)? What in the package compensates for this (longer than normal holiday entitlement? higher salary? a smart car?)? If you are having trouble making up your mind, it may be useful to write a list of points for and against so that you can see how the advantages of the package outweigh the disadvantages (or the other way round).

It is normal to spend up to 48 hours considering an offer, if the job is a permanent position. But this does all depend on what industry you work in and how much pressure there is on the employer to get the position filled. For example, it would be laughable for you to ask for 48 hours to consider a position as a bartender when you walked into the bar having seen a notice in the window and were interviewed ten minutes later.

On the other hand, do not allow a prospective employer to hurry you into making a decision. It would be wrong for both of you to rush in without considering. An ill-considered acceptance can lead to your being very unhappy and resigning after only a brief period. This is bad for you and for the employer for whom high staff turnover can be extremely damaging. Equally, if the employer has offered you the job, he must be pretty sure he wants you and is unlikely to withdraw the offer if you don't respond immediately.

Balancing two offers

If you are extremely lucky, you may be offered two or more jobs at once and be able to trade off one against the other until you get the best deal. When doing this, it is best to be open about what is going on. Tell both recruiters that you are discussing a position with someone else (giving no details). However, avoid bullishness and the arrogance that goes with it.

After the offer

Do not stop attending interviews and applying for jobs until you have closed the deal on the job you have been offered. There's still a chance that something could go wrong at the last minute, so keep your options open as long as you can. If you have other opportunities just waiting for you to explore them, you are less likely to be hussled into a job that is unsuitable. Continue attending interviews even if you are in negotiation, particularly if you have some reservations about the job on offer.

If you have received the offer of a job by post, it is polite to respond by post, although if you have been doing some of the negotiation over the 'phone, it would be natural to relay the news by that method and send a written confirmation in the post. The letter on the facing page is an example.

> *Dear Mrs Jenkins,*
>
> *Thank you for your offer of the position of Stores Manager, detailed in your letter of 29th August.*
> *This is to confirm that I would be delighted to take up the position as described.*
>
> *I am taking a short holiday, but will call you on 5th September to arrange the details of my first day.*
>
> *Yours sincerely,*

If you wish to reject the offer, you must find a credible reason for doing so, and you must explain this reason in your letter. Try to leave the door open. Do not be rude ('I could not bear to work in such a dirty and disorganized office...'), and apologise for your refusal. However, never admit that you have wasted a recruiter's time. The discussions took place on both sides. The decision needed to be made on both sides. You could not possibly have known for certain that you wanted the job until it was described fully.

A suitable letter might go something along the lines of the example on page 176. Most reasonable employers would not be upset by this refusal – it is politely stated and the reason is better than most. If, like this candidate, you manage to turn

Dear Mrs Jenkins

Thank you for your letter dated 16th August and your kind offer of the position of Stores Manager.

I have given the matter a great deal of thought, particularly the probability of long hours that you describe. As you know, I have a young family and share their care with my wife, who also has a full-time job. I am afraid that I am unable to ignore this commitment.

In view of this, I cannot accept your offer at this time. However, if you have an opening that does not require such long hours, or another position that might be suitable, I would be delighted if you would get in touch.

Once again, thank you for your kind offer. I hope that you find a more suitable candidate in the near future.

Yours sincerely

down the offer of a job without burning your bridges, you will have a note in your diary for one month hence to make contact with the recruiter on the off-chance that something suitable has come up.

Correspondence files

As a caution, you should keep all correspondence relating to your job. If you find that the requirements of your employment have been misrepresented to you, the letters may stand up as evidence if you need to attend a tribunal. It could also be used to help 'forgetful' employers recall that they promised you a pay rise after three months, or that they said you could leave work at 3 p.m. on Fridays, for example.

Contractors and freelancers

Of course, for those who are not looking for permanent employment but are seeking clients who can offer them contract work, the process of contact-interview-negotiation is going on more or less all the time.

For contractors and freelancers it is even more important to keep those interview and negotiation skills up to scratch, and to reassess their bargaining position (skills, experience, qualifications exchanged for what you want) regularly. See pages 193–200 for more advice for those who are self-employed.

ADVICE FOR WOMEN RETURNERS

*'Housework is what woman does that nobody notices
unless she hasn't done it.'*

Evan Esar

A feature of the modern work market is the return of women to
paid employment while still bringing up children or caring for
ageing parents or relatives. In 1994, 46% of women with at
least one child below the age of four were working (30% part
time, 16% full time). For women with a youngest child in the
11–15 age bracket, this proportion leapt to 74% (40% part time,
34% full time). This group is fast growing as the population
bump known as the baby-boom moves into the late-30s and
40s age group, and a significant fall in the number of 20s and
teens in the market also takes place. In the last decades, it has
also become more acceptable for women with children to go
out to work. These two things have combined so that now
many women are being released from a lifetime as
'housewives' into a world of opportunity that can seem very
exciting, but also daunting and unfamiliar.

However, many women still take the leading responsibility
for managing the home and dependants such as children and
ageing relatives at the same time as trying to hold down paid
work outside the home. This brings with it special problems.

Building self-confidence

When a woman decides that, for whatever reason, it is time to look for paid employment outside the home, her biggest obstacle is her own attitude to herself, her abilities and skills.

At the outset she may be fighting from a position of weakness – she may already have low self-esteem. This is to be expected if you see a woman's work at home as a job, at which she has suddenly taken a cut in hours (the children are now at school and no longer need the moment-by-moment attention they once did), or has even been made redundant (the children have grown up and gone away). Those who are made redundant after a long period with a single employer often experience confusion and anger – what am I good for, now that they don't need me any more? In a way, mothers whose children have flown the nest, or carers who have been relieved of their task must also feel abandoned and unwanted. After many years spent caring for others, it must be quite a shock to find people no longer need you so much.

Lack of confidence is a second problem. Confidence is to do with familiarity. We are all to a lesser or greater extent, afraid of the unfamiliar. When a person has been away from the work environment for some time, the changes that take place during that break add up so that when she returns, there are many things she thinks she cannot understand or do. In fact, this feeling happens after a very short time away and is almost always an illusion. The initial feeling of inability to cope with a new situation soon disappears.

To build up your self-confidence, start with the self-assessment exercises in chapter 1 (pages 7–26). When you have finished you should have a good idea of what you can do, and what you want to do. Your confidence should already be on the up and up, boosted with the knowledge that you have just as many skills as anyone else, except yours may be a little rusty. Researching the work you think you want to do in the manner discussed in chapter 3 will enable you to confirm your first thoughts and become more certain that you have the basic skills and temperament it takes to do the job.

Train for a better job

Avoid the temptation to settle for the first job that comes along. Many women returners find themselves in jobs with poor pay and conditions and no prospects of promotion because they have little faith in their own skills. Take the time to train for a better job (even if you have to do so at night school while keeping the family going by working part time during the day). Attending a training course could be your first practical step towards returning to the work market. It will also help your self-confidence and increase your network of contacts (vital when it comes to finding a job, see pages 58–61).

Staff at your local Jobcentre will be able to make suggestions and give information on a range of courses that will enable you to brush up your skills or acquire new ones. You will also find information at your local library. A wide range of courses is now available to mature students, from one-day refreshers to Access courses designed to prepare those who have not studied for a number of years to return to full-time education and perhaps earn a degree.

You may also be eligible for grants or benefits if you take up training or education opportunities, so ask either at the Jobcentre or do some research at the library. In some cases, you could be eligible for a one-off scholarship or bursary. Many specialist bodies offer small amounts of money to help out when you are studying, and one of these could pay for the childcare or household help that could make all the difference to your decision. The library should hold a directory of all these bodies, giving their requirements.

Planning

Of course, as a mother or carer, you know what planning is all about, and if you are to go back into paid work, your management skills are going to be stretched. If you still have responsibilities towards children, a partner or others, you will need to work out how you are going to keep the ship afloat. Make a detailed diary of your day-to-day activities and start to rationalize them. Don't try to be superwoman. Work out ways in which you might spend less time cleaning the house (hire a cleaner using part of your wages? ask the children to help out on a rota basis?), cooking (freeze meals to be eaten during the week, buy a slow cooker or a microwave), doing the laundry (use the services of a shirt laundry, or service wash at a laundrette), or all those other things you do regularly to keep things running smoothly.

Decide also how you would be able to make time to honour your commitments: your daughter's gymnastics class, your son's football, or your mother's hospital appointment.

In all of this, you will be at risk of forgetting your own leisure. Don't. You will need as much energy as you can muster, and time spent relaxing will recharge your batteries.

Keeping everyone happy

You will, of course, require the help of your dependants, and you should seek this by emphasizing the good things that are going to come out of your going to work, not just for yourself, but also for them. More money coming in could mean a second television, a holiday, new clothes, wine with meals or even a new house.

At the same time you should be aware that when you turn your attention to other things, your dependants may feel less well-loved or cared-for. Watch for the signs: a resentful or uncommunicative child, a parent or partner demanding attention. Find ways to make them see that you are not abandoning them without exhausting yourself giving in to unreasonable demands.

The main person you will need to get on your side is your partner. Some partners are completely amenable to the changes, but some may feel that if you are not at home to care for their domestic needs, their own work may suffer. You will need to spend quite a lot of time getting to the bottom of any objections and working out ways that they may be countered.

However, do not be made to feel guilty for wanting to start working again. Admit that if you are planning to spend the best part of your week doing other things, the house is never going to look the same, and emergencies may sometimes arise when you can't be there. Your dependants' way of life is going to change, so don't work yourself into the ground trying to maintain past standards.

Finding the right kind of work

When you have worked out that it is possible to juggle everything satisfactorily, and you know what kind of work you want to do (perhaps you have even decided to work at home for a while), start to look for work using the advice given in chapters 1–6. The following notes pick up points that are especially important for returners:

- Temporary or part time work can be a perfect step back into the world of work after a career break, and can be particularly useful if you want to taste a number of jobs or industries before settling on one. The flexibility of temping and working part-time can make it possible for you to do this on-the-job research while still having time for your other responsibilities.
- The job you choose need not be in the same field or industry as the job you had before took your career break. You will have changed and developed since you stopped doing paid work, and you will probably have much more in the way of skills to offer. Take your dreams seriously, and see if you can find a way to break into the work you want to do.
- It is never too late to start. Many companies, seeing the pool of talent represented by women returners, are actively recruiting older women and offering childcare and flexible working packages to enable them to take up places. In these kinds of jobs you are likely to be valued as an ordinary member of staff and there is, in theory, no reason why you should not be on the promotion ladder

after the appropriate training. Equally, the range of educational opportunities for older people has never been greater. Do not allow yourself to believe you are too old.

- The process of researching what the job involves can also fill you in on what has happened in your field since you took your break. Catch up by reading trade newspapers and magazines, and make use of all your contacts to arrange meetings with people who can tell you about recent changes.
- Find a mentor (see page 45) who can give you support and practical help. This may be a relative, friend or neighbour, or someone from a class or women's group. You may both be looking for work at the same time and will find it helpful to share experiences, news of opportunities and help each other brush up writing and interview skills.
- When you are offered a job, it is extremely important that you find out how much others are being paid for the same job in the same industry (see page 134–5). Some employers expect women returners to take low pay in order just to get out of the house. Even if you are working for 'pin money' you owe it to other women in your industry to not lower the average wage by settling for peanuts.

Whatever the circumstances of your career break and your motivations for returning to the work market, there is no reason at all why you should not be able to find a suitable job or arrange for work as a self-employed person, as long as you recognize that your skills and experiences have value, and that with energy and planning you could enrich your own life and that of those around you.

ADVICE FOR OLDER WORKERS

*'Change is not made without inconvenience,
even from worse to better.'*

Richard Hooker (c.1554–1600)

For many people who have worked all their lives, perhaps in the same company, the spectre of redundancy or mandatory early retirement nowadays looms large. As companies slim down to skeletal proportions, retaining only a core of administrative staff, more and more older managers and executives are finding that their services are no longer required.

Combatting shock

When this happens to you, the first thing to be aware of is that you are in shock. Any change in your lifestyle is a small shock to your mental and physical system. As we get older, we all get used to doing things a certain way. If you have been following the same routine for 20 years, imagine how your body and brain is going to react when all of a sudden this stops and the routine changes.

Of course, gradually you will get used to not going to work, but in the meantime, understand that your mind and your body are trying to cope with the change. All sorts of symptoms may occur: mood swings, irritability, depression, inability to sleep; a succession of small health problems like colds and 'flu.

To combat the effects of all this, stick to your routine.

Chapter 2 (pages 27–47) discusses methods of planning your search for work and emphasizes the fact that this search should be seen as a job in itself. Get up in the mornings and dress as if you were going to work, and then make use of your lifetime routine to propel yourself into your search for work.

Furthermore, it is important to eat sensibly and regularly, and to keep fit. If you are not already in a fitness regime, it would be useful to start (at a gentle pace to begin with, and ask your doctor's advice first). Not only will increased fitness help to ward off depression and many little physical ailments, it will also make you appear to be more youthful and more employable when interview time comes around.

Advantages enjoyed by older workers

It is true to say that those who find themselves in the job market later in life are more vulnerable than, say, the young second-jobber. There has been strong discrimination in favour of younger people, but, in fact, recruiters who discriminate in this way are running the risk of losing excellent staff, and some are coming round to this way of thinking. As time goes on, and the population becomes older, fewer young people will be available. So, in theory at least, it should become easier for the fifty-something worker to find work. At the same time, you as an older person have some advantages in the work market that youngsters do not:

- Over the years you must have picked up hundreds of contacts. This is a resource worth its weight in gold, and one that no twenty-something is likely to have.

- Statistically, you are likely to be more loyal than the average youngster, more likely to stay in the job once trained and more likely to be conscientious and reliable. These points can be made to the employer in favour of employing you.
- You have decades of experience, and if you can break down those experiences into tasks you have successfully carried out, you should have a list as long as your arm of the things you can offer a potential employer (see pages 12–19).
- You have a wide range of knowledge about work and about the work market. You know who the employers are in your field, and what the various jobs entail. You know which of these jobs you can do – and there should be more than one. At the same time, your many skills and experiences should open up a wide range of doors for you to choose from.
- You understand the language of your business. You can speak to the interviewer from a position of knowledge and understanding, as colleague to colleague rather than employer to recruitment candidate. You are an insider by dint of your many years in the business. Show that you can fit in to the employer's set-up.

Start from a position of strength

The best situation you could be in when searching for work at this stage in your life is working. It is vital, therefore, that you scent the changes in the wind, and start to look for new sources of work *before* you are handed your marching papers.

There are two strategies you could adopt if you are still in work and looking for a way to avoid redundancy.

First, simply start a work search as if you were out of work, asking contacts for information on opportunities, watching the national newspapers for advertisements and starting to make discreet speculative advances towards possible employers.

On the other hand, you could make use of your insider knowledge of your own company either to make it possible to move to a new role that is not threatened by redundancy, or to offer your services on a freelance or contract basis. In both of these cases, you will need to analyse your company to discover where the safe jobs are or what problem needs to be solved. Keep your eyes open for things going wrong or things going well. Pay attention to company newsletters and other sources of general information. When you have hit upon a problem area inside your company, frame a proposal for the solution in such a way as to make your company say 'yes' to your solving it for them.

All companies have warts: areas in which they have pressures they cannot cope with, problems of technology or manpower they don't seem to be able to solve. Find out where these problems are and get your ideas down on paper. Discuss your solution with your superiors, and argue that you are the ideal person to implement it. This may mean that you actually give up your employed status to contract your services back to the company (and at a higher price if you are smart) on a project-by-project basis. And this may leave you free to offer your services to other companies as well.

Whether you remain employed but in a different role, or you

persuade your employers to use you as a contractor, you are safe from the grim blade of redundancy, and if you continue to make yourself useful by actively searching out problems and devising solutions, you should reap the benefits long into the future.

Making a major change

Before plunging into all of these defensive and offensive activities, work through the self-assessment exercises in chapter 1. You may find that you would actually prefer to let your current career go for some reason. You may want to start your own business based on a former hobby, or join a friend in her new enterprise. Perhaps you are close to retirement and the sea-change that this time of life brings with it.

Be open to suggestions of work that you had not thought of. It is very easy to begin to believe that we can do only one thing, to limit our horizons. But just because we have been doing that one thing for the past ten years or so, does not mean we can't do something else. And sometimes it takes someone else to see the opportunity for you. At your time of life, you should be able to use your experience in many different situations. Enterprising managers will value these skills, and may even design a role specifically for you. If a serious suggestion or offer does not fit all your criteria, negotiate.

Keep your mind open also to new opportunities outside the sphere you have hitherto worked in. If your children have grown up and moved away, you may realise that you are free at last to take some risks and have some fun in your working life. Perhaps part-time work as a contractor would leave you free to devote more time to volunteer work. You may even decide to join VSO (Voluntary Service Overseas, see page 207–8), or a similar organization, and export your skills to needy countries around the world.

Age discrimination

In our society it is still true that we expect older people to be more senior in their professional lives. This sometimes comes across as a difficulty some managers have in telling older people what is wanted in the job, and directing their ongoing work. In the world of education, it often takes a while to get used to a student who is 50, for example, because it is expected that he should have done all his learning when he was younger. But if the influx of older people back into higher education is anything to go by, our views on older people are changing, and gradually we will all become more comfortable with the idea that learning continues throughout life and that the person who starts a new career in mid-life, perhaps at the bottom of the ladder, has not necessarily failed.

These preconceptions can also work the other way around, in a situation where an older employee resents being directed by a youngster. If the older worker is aware that he or she has such feelings, any problems arising can be solved through open discussion between the manager and the worker.

Unhappily, though, the remnants of our beliefs about older people could still affect your chances of success at interview. Here are some notes to think about when preparing for the big day:

- While your many years in the industry enable you to speak with some authority, avoid sounding like a know-all. All companies are slightly different, so show that you expect a period of learning (if not actual training). Make it clear that you understand you would be going into a new situation and that you know you may have to alter your thinking in order to bring all your skills and experience to bear.

- In most cases, the employer is looking for someone who will fit into the company and will do things their way. You will need to emphasize your flexibility in this respect. While most companies value innovation, most are wary of change. Show that you are capable of creative thinking, but do not be quick to suggest sweeping changes. Avoid saying things like, 'when I was at xyz company, we did things this way...'
- Show that you are able to take direction from a younger person. If you are an older man who has been working for a very traditional employer in the past, you may need to come to terms with the fact that your boss could not only be younger than you, but she could also be a woman.
- Do not make a big thing about your age when talking to contacts or recruiters. Avoid drawing attention to your age using phrases such as: '...when I was training, 30 years ago...' or '...of course, in my day...' This is still your day, and if you have not been on a training course since 1965, you should perhaps think about doing so! Do not put your age on your CV.
- The saying that you can't teach an old dog new tricks may be absolutely false, but many people still believe that it is

true. Keep up with advances in technology and be prepared to retrain.

For those who believe that after a period of hard work in your early career, later life is simply a freewheel down the hill to a golden retirement, redundancy can come as a huge shock to the mental, physical and financial system. However, the opportunity it provides to get out of the rut and start something new is also golden, provided you can muster the energy and imagination to take the leap.

CONTRACT AND HOME WORKING

'Everyone lives by selling something.'
                    Robert Louis Stevenson (1850–1894)

In 1980–81 6.1% of the population of the UK were registered as being self-employed. Eleven years later, in 1993, that figure had risen to 8.3%, and by 1994, a total of almost 3.3 million people were self-employed (12.9% of those in employment). Of all those people in the UK working, about 650,000 are now working at home, and one quarter of those are managers and administrators (source: Social Trends 25: 1994).

As companies pare down their staff, employing fewer people full time but calling on skills on a project-by-project basis, the number of people opting for self-employment will inevitably rise. This trend is taking place at the same time as communications technology is taking leaps and bounds towards the sci-fi world of the 21st-century telecommunity. Physical documents, electronic information and verbal messages can all be transmitted within seconds from all over the world, so it is theoretically possible for a company to employ homeworkers in many different locations. The only thing that holds back this revolution is the reluctance of workers to leave behind the social aspects of office life, and the fear of managers that workers will not work or work properly without constant direction and watchfulness.

Self-employment can take a variety of forms, but the

common denominator is that in theory the self-employed person controls the tasks she carries out and is in practice responsible for her own tax and national insurance contributions. In theory, too, she has a number of clients to whom she sells her products or services.

Being self-employed can be very exciting, and the flexibility it implies can solve a number of practical problems such as planning your working day around children or restricted mobility. If your service or product is in demand, you can choose who you work for (and for how much), and what kinds of projects you become involved in. Changing projects from day to day, month to month or year to year can keep you on your toes, and ensures that you gain a wide range of experience.

Apart from the skills you are using to sell your product or service (your skill as a painter if you are setting up as a painter and decorator, for example), you will need a number of others to keep your business going. You will need to learn how to keep proper records, particularly when it comes to money, and how to draw up financial projections and business plans. You will need to learn how to complete necessary secretarial tasks such as writing letters and filing information, making appointments and arranging travel. You will also need to learn how to market your product or service, and how to keep yourself motivated to carry on working without any outside force.

If you have followed the advice given in this book you should already have begun to learn a number of these skills:

- Setting up your work-search headquarters (see pages 28–30), an area of your home from which to conduct your search, is a step towards arranging a home office (see below).

- Researching companies that might employ you requires the same skills as researching companies or other customers that would probably buy your service or product.
- Making speculative applications to possible employers is similar to approaching a possible client and telling him about your product or service.
- Analysing a company's performance in an effort to find out what problems it has that you might be able to solve is just one step in deciding what product or service is likely to be successful.

Notes for homeworkers

Many self-employed people make use of their own homes from which to run their business. While there are obvious financial savings to be made, there are many pitfalls to be avoided. Most of these come from the fact that your workspace is within your living space, and the distinction between work and leisure becomes blurred. The following pointers will help you be aware of potential problems:

- As you did with your work-search headquarters, set aside a place dedicated to your work, preferably a whole room (with a door that closes) – avoid working on the kitchen or dining-room table. Even if your business entails designing and knitting sweaters at home, you will still need not only space in which to do the production, but also an area in which to administer your business. You will need a desk and a filing cabinet, a telephone and a typewriter or word-processor at the very least.

- If you have expensive equipment such as specialized computers and printers, think about extra insurance. If you intend to work from home, check your policy to ensure that you are still adequately covered, and to ensure that your policy is not invalidated if you work at home, as some are.

- 'Go to work' just as you would as if you were leaving for the office. Set aside particular times for breaks and finish work at a given time. You need not work normal office hours, though if you work closely with staff in offices you may have to agree a 'core time' at which you overlap with your contacts. Most of us have certain times of the day at which we are most productive, and the advantages of working during those times are obvious. Avoid if at all possible the temptation to work long hours. If you are being offered more work than you can handle, pay someone else to do it. If the work continues to grow, you will naturally employ more and more people, eventually becoming a booming small business.

- Dress as if you were going to work. Don't work in your dressing gown.

- Make sure that other members of your household understand that when you are in your workspace, you are working and should not be disturbed. It is almost impossible to work effectively when you are constantly being interrupted, especially by the demands of babies and small children. If this may be the case, think about engaging a child minder and make sure that he or she knows that, even though you are in the house you should only be disturbed in an emergency.

- Keep your workspace tidy and clean.
- If you live alone, working from home can become very lonely. Make plans to get out and see friends or to telephone friends and colleagues. Try to make contact with the outside world at least once a day. If you are keeping up your network of contacts (see pages 59–61), you should have plenty of people to keep in touch with.

Testing the waters

Many people leave permanent work to continue working on a freelance basis. Among these are women who want to have children or people who want to leave the hell of the daily commute behind and live the quiet life away from the city. Indeed, the rural areas of the UK have the highest numbers of self-employed people (in 1994, for example, Powys recorded 36% of its population as being self-employed). The majority of these people do the same job but for a number of clients and are based at home. In other cases, the self-employed person will start a completely new business, perhaps based on a hobby that started to make money of its own accord.

Continuing to do a job you have done previously is a relatively safe way of going self-employed. However, if you wish to start something completely new, you will need to test the waters first. Don't give up your old job (if you have one) until you are certain that your idea can be turned into a going concern:

- Talk to contacts in the business you intend to move into. Get an idea of how much you can sell your product or service for, and the methods being used by those already in the business. Build up your network and continue to work at it – self-employed people can very easily 'disappear' if they don't stay in touch, not only with their current clients, but also with former colleagues and acquaintances.
- Research customers and clients. Get in touch with them using the technique for speculative applications. Before sending off those letters, be absolutely sure that the company could use your service and that you have the name of the person who makes the decisions.
- Make an inventory of your own skills. Remember that you will need to administer your business as well as do the work. You may need to attend a course at your local adult education centre to learn the basics of business management. *Collins Pocket Reference Office Organizer* is a complete guide to office organization and skills, and is written with the young business in mind.
- Use all available sources of help and advice. The Jobcentre can give you advice about starting in business – you may be eligible for extra benefits or a local authority grant, or you may find you could benefit from a local government, central government, or even EC, initiative. Your bank may also be able to help you with a business plan or with market research.
- Be prepared for your business to change as it grows. Contacts may suggest changes in what you do or in the product you supply. If this happens, consider the wider

market and not just the single client. Would the change be acceptable to your other customers, could you widen your market by making the change? On-going research about your market is vital, and flexibility is a watchword of the self-employed.

When your initial research is complete you should be able to answer the following questions:

- What is your product or service? Define it exactly.
- Who do you intend to sell your product or service to? Is your market local, national or international? Is your market large or is it a specialist market? Will you sell to just one customer or will you need to find a large number of customers.
- What are the skills you will need in order to make your product or perform your service? Do you need to train in areas that you are not already conversant with (selling, marketing, administration)?
- What equipment are you going to need? Do you know how to use it? And maintain it?
- Do you need an initial investment (for example, a loan from the bank or a lump sum taken from your savings) to start your business?
- Are there any laws that you will have to find out about and comply with? Examples are planning permission for change of use if you are setting up at home, tax law, health and safety regulations.

Finding work as a self-employed person is often not easy, and making a success of it as a long-term method of earning an adequate and stable income is even harder. Don't be afraid to make changes if things don't work out. If nothing else, your experience out on your own will have provided some valuable and positive insights into your own skills and temperament, which can be used in your on-going search for work.

LOOKING FOR WORK ABROAD

'To travel hopefully is a better thing than to arrive, and the true success is to labour.'

Robert Louis Stevenson (1850–1894)

Most people at some time or another take a look out of the window onto a typically grey and dreary winter day and long to be working abroad: the Mediterranean, the Gulf, anywhere warm and sunny; New York, Paris, Los Angeles, wherever the 'creative' people are; Australia, New Zealand, where people know how to enjoy life; the exotic Far East. Indeed approaching a quarter of a million Britons go abroad to work every year. Some stay away for only a short time. Others never come back.

Working abroad is not for everybody, and before you start to search, you will need to decide whether you are the kind of person who could survive in a foreign country. You will also have to work out what you really want out of your sojourn abroad and how it will fit into the rest of your life:

- Would you do the job you are doing at home in a foreign country? Would you embark on a different kind of work? For example, many people travel abroad to teach English regardless of their profession at home. Would you need to be employed, or could you be self-employed?
- What are the immigration requirements for your country of choice? UK nationals are now entitled to live and work

in any country belonging to the EC. Outside the EC different regulations apply. Some Commonwealth countries operate exchange programmes giving young UK nationals work permits for certain periods of time. Other countries require that you have a firm contract from the employing company before they will issue a work permit. Contact the country's consulate for details of regulations.

- Do you have dependants? How would you organize them? Would you leave your family at home and return on leave periodically? Would you take your family with you? If the latter is the case, what are the ramifications for your children's education? How will they cope with a change of language? Would the period abroad disrupt your partner's plans? If your partner were to accompany you, would he or she wish to work, and what would he or she do?

- What position would you be in when you return home to stay? Will you be able to slot back into your old job? This is probably expected if you have been sent abroad by your company. However, if you decide to look for a new job abroad, you may also find yourself hunting for work on your return. How much money will you have to cushion your return? This depends on how long you think it will take you to find work on your return.

- What will you do with your property while you are away? Can you let your house or flat? Will you put your furniture and other possessions in storage, or will you take everything with you? Will you have somewhere to stay when you get off the aeroplane? Will the company accommodate you? Where will that accommodation be and what will it consist of?

- What are the tax implications of your working abroad? Will you pay tax in your host country, or will you still be liable in the UK?
- Will you be paid in the local currency? Is that currency 'hard', will it convert easily into sterling. Could you be paid in sterling? What is the host country's economic state? Is there high inflation? What standard of living would your salary bring? Would you be able to take your earnings out of the country?
- What effect will your period abroad have on your pension scheme at home?
- Do you speak the language? Will you need to learn? What is the minimum fluency you will need to start working, and how will you arrange lessons when you arrive?
- Is the host country politically stable? Does it have a good record on crime, particularly crimes of violence. If not, you might think again about your personal safety.
- Are there any possible health hazards? What are health facilities like? This is particularly important if you are planning to take children with you, or if you have an illness that requires regular attention.
- What is the climate of the country you are planning to work in? Do you know whether you will be able to cope with the extreme heat of the tropics or the twilight days of the Scandinavian winter?
- Does your chosen destination have religious or legal

restrictions that you think you would find intolerable. Some countries prohibit the drinking of alcohol, others have strict dress codes for women.

Routes to working abroad

Finding work abroad can be done using all the routes and techniques described in chapters 1–6. Researching the market in your country of choice will be a little more specialized: you may need to visit a library specializing in business information (your librarian can advise), and contacts who actually work in your target country and, perhaps company, may be few.

Some national newspapers, and most trade magazines advertise positions abroad. It also is possible to buy foreign newspapers in the UK. Your newsagent should be able to advise.

The Jobcentre can give you access to the Employment Service's Overseas Placing Unit, which can offer help and advice and keeps a limited register of vacancies. The Department of Trade and Industry can offer information on how your qualifications compare against those of other countries. Some recruitment consultancies specialize in placing applicants in jobs abroad.

If you decide that you want to make speculative approaches to companies abroad, carry on the task as if you were approaching companies in this country. However, if your chosen country is not Anglophone, you will get nowhere unless you write your application in the local language. You might need a translator to help you do this, and the Yellow Pages will yield phone numbers.

Vet the employer

This is a golden rule and applies across the board. Always check out the employing company. Look them up in the business directories to be found in the reference section of the local library. Ask around. Find out who they are and what their standing is in the community, both national and international. Of course, if your prospective employer is a well-known multinational there is less need for caution, and if the job you are chasing is advertised in a national newspaper in the UK, you can be more or less sure that it has been vetted by the newspaper itself. Be particularly cautious about obscure companies, and even more so if they offer salaries or returns on investment that are sky high. In general, avoid agencies that ask to be paid to place you in a job abroad, particularly if they operate from countries overseas.

Even if your employing company is a multinational, make sure that you have a contract (preferably covered by English law), and get the contract assessed by a legal expert. While you will certainly have to pay to do this, it is essential that you are contractually secure. The contract should cover every item of your employment, including such matters as:

- Salary, currency, method of payment.
- Period of the contract and notice periods.
- Severance pay.
- Hours of work, place of work, etc.
- Contribution to your pension.
- Tax arrangements.
- Travel arrangements: what will the company pay for in

terms of return trips? What will the company pay for as regards your dependants' travel? What will the company contribute to your relocation both to the host country and back home at the end of the contract.

- Holiday entitlements.
- Arrangements for education and training: language training, your children's education, language training for your partner, vocational training.
- Domestic arrangements: who pays for your accommodation, household staff, day-to-day transport?

Travelling speculatively

It may be that when you set off for the far horizon you have no job to go to but intend to look for work on arrival. You might be a freelancer, or perhaps a student more intent on seeing the world than on working. If this is the case, it is a good idea to take two precautions:

- Think about what skills you have and try to find out how easy it will be to sell them. For example, you may speak English, but to teach English you will probably need to show a TEFL qualification. Do you really have skills that you could rely on to support you? Or will you need to get some before you leave? If you intend to freelance, make contact with possible clients before you leave.
- Budget your trip carefully. Leave some money at home for your return or for emergencies during your trip. Decide how long you have before you need to start making money to support yourself while abroad. Give yourself a

deadline and stick to it. If possible avoid being caught without cash in a foreign country.

The volunteer option

If you want to travel overseas and lend your skills to a developing country, Voluntary Service Overseas (VSO) may be a good way to do it. VSO supplies qualified people to a wide range of countries in a wide range of skills. The 'volunteer' is employed by an agency of the host country, and a large proportion of the job he is required to do is training in-country staff. The volunteer is paid by the host country in the currency of that country and at local rates. Many normal expatriates enjoy a high standard of living while in developing countries, because they are paid salaries equivalent to that which they would receive at home in a country where the cost of living is significantly lower. VSO volunteers are paid at local rates and live in more or less the same way as local people. Contracts are for a minimum of two years, and the interview and selection process is rigorous. However, VSO can be recommended because of the expert support offered to the volunteer in the field and the systems established to cushion the blow when the volunteer returns home.

VSO advertises opportunities in the national press, but if you do not see a specific job advertised, apply speculatively. The position for you may just have come through. And don't think that because you are at retirement age you will not be accepted. VSO actively prefers to take people with valuable experience and skills, and that is exactly what you have.

Working abroad can open up horizons a person never new existed. It can also be extremely difficult, and many try for a short time and find they are not suited to life in foreign climes. Overcoming culture shock and homesickness are the most common problems, and these should not be underestimated: they return again and again, even to expatriates who have been abroad for many years. However, if you have the opportunity to go abroad, and the courage to do so, good luck and bon voyage!

A-Z OF WORK-RELATED TERMS

Apprenticeship
Hands-on vocational training organized by the employer, particularly in a trade (such as printing or engineering). The period of apprenticeships can vary, and at one time could be as much as seven or ten years). Nowadays, three years is usual, and that time often includes college-based study on block-release leading to a vocational qualification.

Career break
Period during which a person is not in paid work. This may be for a wide range of reasons. You may have decided to travel, or to bring up a family, to study or to pursue other goals. You may also have been through a period of sickness, unemployment or imprisonment. Use the term on your CV instead of 'unemployed' to make it sound more positive.

Career development loan
Scheme whereby those who wish to undertake a course of education or training related to their work prospects can get a loan. Over the period of the training, the government pays the interest on the loan, and the student does not need to start repayments of the capital (and any other interest) until the course is completed. The local Jobcentre can advise.

Citizens Advice Bureau (CAB)

Network of organizations that keep walk-in offices in most towns. CAB offers advice, mostly free of charge, on all areas, particularly to do with the law, housing, the benefits system, etc. You may need advice on your contract of employment, or help filling out complicated forms, or you may wish to find out what your rights are in a certain situation. If the bureau cannot advise you on the spot, they will try to find a specialist to help you. Your local office is listed in the telephone directory.

Commission

Payment according to results. Those most commonly found to be on commission are sales people. Many work with a small fixed salary and augment it with commission. Those on commission only are likely to give you the hardest sell!

Compassionate leave

Time off to deal with events such as deaths or serious illness in the family.

Constructive dismissal

If an employer changes the terms of an employee's contract, and the employee does not agree to the new terms, the employee can resign his job and then make a claim for constructive dismissal.

Core time

In a flexitime (see below) system, the core time is the period of time during which an employee is expected to be at work. The core time is organized so that the people who need to communicate with each other are at work at the same time to enable this to happen. If you are working at home, you may adjust your working times in the same way, but it is useful to identify a core time at which you should be available for telephone calls and visits on a regular basis.

Correspondence course
Course of study pursued at home rather than in the classroom or lecture hall. Tutors and students communicate through correspondence, and the course is based on self-study. It is useful to take a correspondence course if your local college does not offer the subjects you want, but studying alone is hard work, requiring a high level of self-motivation. Check the credentials of the college before parting with money.

Covering letter
A letter that is sent with other enclosures. The job-hunter is expected to send a covering letter with a CV or application form. See pages 105–113.

Curriculum vitae
Latin for 'the road of life'. The curriculum vitae is a document in which the job-hunter lists education and employment history and highlights skills and achievements. The CV is one of the most important documents most people will ever have to put together, because it is used to assess abilities, background and experience. See pages 82–105.

Employment agency

Private company that places workers in temporary, part-time or permanent work. The agency is paid by the employer, and not by the worker. Names and telephone numbers are to be found in the Yellow Pages. See page 635.

Employment Protection (Consolidation) Act 1978

The Act of Parliament that covers most general aspects of employment, including contracts, dismissal, maternity rights, trades unions, etc. Self-employed people are not protected by the provisions of this act.

Equal opportunities

Philosophy that encourages businesses to consider all their employees (and potential employees) as equal regardless of race, gender, religion, sexual orientation or disability. A company that claims it is an 'equal opportunities employer' (in a job advertisement, for example) is conscious of discrimination and has tried to reduce it.

Equal Pay Act (1970)

Act of Parliament that ensures equality of pay between people doing substantially the same kind of job or jobs that are worth the same. The Act was originally enacted to bring women's pay more into line with men's.

Executive search and placement service

Alternative name for a headhunter (see below).

Expatriate

Person who goes abroad to live and work. Some expatriates are away from their homeland for one or two years only, but others never come back!

Fee

Payment of a fixed sum for a job done. This contrasts with salaries or wages, which are based on the amount of time worked, or with piecework, which is paid by the number of items produced or processed.

Flexitime

Time-keeping system in which employees agree to work a fixed minimum number of hours per month. A core period is fixed (see above), but outside that time period, the employee can come and go within reason, so long as the minimum is observed. If the employee works more hours, they can be added together to give 'flexidays', which she takes as holiday. Flexitime is particularly useful for parents who need to see their children to school or for others who find it difficult to fit into the usual nine-to-five routine.

Franchise

A situation in which a company authorizes another (or a self-employed person) to sell its goods and services in a particular area. The 'parent' company often supplies staff training, display and promotional material and the goods, and the franchisee pays a fee.

Graphology

The inference of a person's character through his or her handwriting. When recruiting very senior staff, some companies will turn to a graphologist to help decide whether a candidate is suitable. However, most companies also use other assessment methods alongside this one.

Gross misconduct

Unacceptable behaviour on the part of an employee, including stealing and fighting.

Headhunter

Firm that specializes in finding high-level or high-profile staff for prosperous companies. Headhunters usually operate through the grapevine, and many positions filled by headhunters are never openly advertised. See pages 64.

Homeworker

A person who does their job at home. Some homeworkers simply require a desk and a telephone, others have to convert part of their house into a studio, office or workshop. See pages 193–200.

Jobcentre

Government-run centre at which local vacancies are advertised and at which job-hunters can arrange interviews or seek specific employment related advice from employment law and the employee's rights to free vocational training.

Jobclub

Government-backed initiative in which those who have been out of work for a long period attend the 'club', which is essentially a self-help group. A leader gives help and advice, but it is up to the members to find jobs. They are helped with free stationery, stamps and office equipment and derive support from the leader and other members. Recent figures show that more than 70% of those attending a Jobclub find work within 12 weeks, and in 1994, more than 100,000 people found a job through the scheme.

Job description

Document that describes the tasks to be carried out by the person in a particular job. Some employers send job descriptions to applying candidates along with application forms. See also job specification.

Job fair

Event that takes place at a university, college or other venue, at which employers invite those looking for work to make contact and find out what positions are or could be available.

Job sharing

System of part-time working in which two people take responsibility for the same job. One person may work mornings, while the other takes over in the afternoons, for example. The system was introduced by many companies (particularly in the public sector) as part of an equal opportunities commitment, to enable mothers to work part-time.

Job specification

Document that describes the person a recruiter is looking for in terms of skills, education, etc. A manager may draw up a job specification for the use of personnel staff when requesting a new member of staff, and recruitment consultants and employment agencies would require a job specification before starting to look for a suitable candidate. See also job description (above).

Lay off

If business is not going well, an employer may opt to tell workers not to come to work. During the time that workers are laid off in this way, they do not receive pay. If employees are laid off for more than four weeks, they are entitled to redundancy pay.

Manufacturing industry

Industry in which companies make things for sale. Compare service industry (below).

Maternity rights

Women who are expecting a baby and have been working for the same employer for a certain period of time are entitled to rights including time off for ante-natal classes and paid leave before and after the child is born.

Milk round

Round of visits made by employers to universities to interview graduating students. See page 64–5.

National Insurance (NI)

The system by which everybody in the UK pays contributions towards the National Health Service and the benefits system. If you are on PAYE, contributions should be deducted from your wages or salary before it reaches you. Your employer is liable to pay further contributions on your behalf. If you are self-employed, you must pay the contributions yourself. You will be asked to pay a regular amount each month, and when your tax liability is assessed for the year, you will be asked to pay a further earnings-related sum. Failure to pay NI contributions could jeopardize your eligibility for state pension or other benefits.

Networking

Making contacts far and wide. A strong network is probably the most valuable asset in any job-search. See pages 58–61.

Open learning

Course of study that allows the maximum of flexibility. Students can study at their own pace and wherever they want (at home, at college, etc.).

Outplacement

Helping workers who are about to be made redundant to reassess their skills and find other work. Many companies are now employing specialist outplacement firms to advise and direct those adversely affected by corporate restructuring.

PAYE

Acronym for pay-as-you-earn, this is the system in which those who are not self-employed have their tax and National Insurance contributions deducted at source.

Piecework

Type of work in which the worker is paid not by the numbers of hours or days worked but by the number of items (pieces) produced or processed. For example, fabric pieces cut out for a clothes manufacturer, objects put together, envelopes stuffed. Those contemplating piecework should beware of hidden costs (heating and lighting if you are working at home, postage and stationery, etc.).

Private sector

The sector that includes companies owned by private citizens. These include public limited companies (plc) as well as limited companies, partnerships (firms) and sole traders.

Psychometric test

Test used by employers or recruitment consultants and headhunters to assess abilities, personality, motivations, intellectual capability.

Public sector

The sector that includes institutions funded by the nation, such as local government, the health service, the civil service, but also schools, colleges, universities and nationalized industries. See also private sector (above).

Recruitment consultant

Company that seeks and screens candidates for jobs on behalf of the employer. See pages 61-3.

Referee

A person who recommends a person to a prospective employer by way of a reference (see below).

Reference

Written or oral statement made by a referee to a potential employer, and designed to give the employer further information about the candidate for the job.

Self-employed

A person who is self-employed effectively runs her own business. She organizes her own time, pays her own tax and NI contributions, and probably has a number of customers or clientrs rather than a single employer.

Service industry

Industry in which companies offer a service for sale rather than an object. For example, estate agents, bankers, travel agents, retailers, office cleaners, teachers, health workers and secretaries are all in the service sector. See also manufacturing industry (above).

Sex discrimination

Treating an employee differently because of his or her gender. If you think you have been the victim of sex discrimination, talk immediately to Citizens Advice (see above), who will be able to advise you.

Sexual harrassment

Unwanted attention of a sexual nature. Members of both sexes can be victims of sexual harrassment, and if you think you may have a case, contact Citizens Advice at once for help. The urgency involved is due to the fact that all actions for sexual harrassment must be brought within a certain time. If you have not begun your action before the time limit expires, you will be disqualified.

Short-time working

If an employer finds that there is not enough work to keep his staff employed, he may opt to reduce the number of hours they work. This is known as short-time working.

Speculative application

Approaching potential employer and telling her about your skills and objectives in the hope that she may have a job for you or may keep your records on file until something suitable comes up. See pages 67–71.

Teleworking

Method of working in which the employee is not present at the employer's office, but communicates using the latest communications technology, such as the Internet, fax, telephone, etc. Teleworking cuts out the time, money and energy wasted on the daily commute and enables workers to be more flexible with their time. For example, many travelling sales people now telework using sophisticated portable computer systems and telephone lines to process orders and pass reports back to the head office.

Temp
Person who is employed on a temporary basis. See pages 71–2.

Testimonial
Open letter of reference, written by a previous employer and handed to the worker for use when talking to possible employers.

Vocational training
Training with a specific job in mind. Vocational training is often compared to academic education, which teaches mental skills and passes on information, but does not train the student to do a particular job. Vocational training is now underpinned by the NVQ (National Vocational Qualifications) system, through which employees can prove skills they have been taught at work and transfer them to other jobs when they move.

VSO (Voluntary Service Overseas)
Organization that places workers in jobs abroad, mostly in developing countries. See page 207.

Youth Training
Scheme to help young people get the training they need to get a job and to progress in their chosen career.

LIST OF OCCUPATIONS

*'The ugliest trades have their moments of pleasure. Now, if
I were a grave-digger, or even a hangman, there are some
people I could work for with a great deal of enjoyment.'*
                              D.W. Jerrold (1803–1857)

When contemplating entering the world of work for the first
time, or when looking around for a completely new direction,
finding out what your options are is a good place to start. We all
have some idea of where our interests lie, and after reading the
early chapters of this book, you should have a good idea of
what field you would like to work in.

The following classified list of occupations is designed as a
first step towards some new ideas. The classifications used are
based on those developed as the Careers Library Classification
Order, and used to catalogue careers publications. The classifications are as follows:

- Administration, business, clerical work and management
- Armed forces
- Art and design
- Educational, cultural, academic occupations
- Theatre, film, entertainment and leisure
- Catering and other services
- Health and medical occupations
- Social and related occupations
- Law and related occupations

- Security and other protective services
- Finance and related occupations
- Buying, selling and related occupations
- Sciences, mathematics and related occupations
- Engineering
- Manufacturing and crafts
- Construction and related occupations
- Work with animals, plants and nature
- Transport and communications

Administration, business, clerical work and management

Accommodation manager	Keyboard operator
Bi-lingual secretary	Local government administrator
Box office assistant	
Civil service admini-strator	Manager
	Management consultant
Company secretary	Medical secretary
Computer operator	Office manager
Data input technician	Patent agent
Health and safety officer	Personal assistant
Health service manager	Personnel officer
Information officer	Post-room worker

LIST OF OCCUPATIONS

Publications officer

Public relations officer

Secretary

Telephonist

Time management consultant

Training officer

Armed forces

Army non-commissioned officer

Army officer

Army private

Royal Air Force officer

Royal Air Force airman/airwoman

Royal Marine

Royal Navy officer

Royal Navy rating

Art and design

Artist's agent

Animator

Cartoonist

Costume designer

Design studio manager

Draughtsman

Fashion designer

Graphic designer

Illustrator

Interior designer

Jewellery designer

Life model

Make-up artist

Packaging designer

Painter

Photographer

Product designer

Sculptor

Set designer

Signwriter

Tattooist

Technical illustrator

Textiles designer

Type designer

Typographer

Educational, cultural, academic occupations

Anthropologist

Archaeologist

Archivist

Art restorer

Arts administrator

Author

Choirmaster

Composer

Conference organizer

Curator

Editor

Genealogist

Indexer

Interpreter/translator

Journalist

Lecturer

Librarian

Literary agent

Picture researcher

Playgroup leader

Poet

Proofreader

Radio journalist

Schools examiner

Sports commentator

Teacher

Technical writer

Theatre, film, entertainment and leisure

Actor

Actor's agent

Athlete

Audio tape editor

Busker

Camera operator

Casting director

Choreographer

Cinema manager

Cinema projectionist

Cinema usher

Circus performer

Continuity person

Croupier

Dancer

Diving instructor

Film/TV/Radio producer

Film/TV/Radio director

Fitness instructor

Leisure centre manager

Lighting technician

Musician

Nightclub DJ

Orchestra conductor

Orchestra manager

Orchestral librarian

Puppeteer

Radio DJ

Radio presenter

Roadie

Singer

Ski instructor

Songwriter

Sports trainer

Sound recordist

Sound technician/editor

Stage manager

Theatre front-of-house manager

Travel agent

Travel representative

Video editor

Vision mixer

Wardrobe staff

Catering and other services

Airline cabin crew

Bar worker

Beautician/beauty therapist

Carpet fitter

Caterer

Cellarman

Chef

Chamberstaff

Chimney sweep

Cleaner

Confectioner

Cook

Dry cleaning worker

Embalmer

Florist

Food service assistant

Funeral director

Hair stylist

Hotel manager

Housekeeper

Laundry worker

Masseur

Messenger/courier

Nanny

Piano tuner

Porter

Publican

Purser

Receptionist

Refuse collector

Restaurant manager

School matron

Stores person

Waiter

Window cleaner

Health and medical occupations

Acupuncturist

Ambulance crew

Art therapist

Auxiliary nurse

Cardiologist

Child psychologist

Chiropodist

Chiropractor

Clinical psychologist

Cosmetic surgeon

Dental hygienist

Dental nurse

Dentist

Dermatologist

Dietician

Drama therapist

Educational psychologist

Epidemiologist

Environmental health officer

General practitioner

Health visitor

Homeopath

Medical herbalist

Midwife

Music therapist

Naturopath

Nurse

Occupational therapist

Ocularist

Optician

Osteopath

Pathologist

Pharmacist

Physiotherapist

Psychologist

Psychotherapist

Radiographer

Residential care assistant

Speech therapist

Surgeon

Social and related occupations

Care assistant

Careers officer

Charity administrator

Charity worker

Community worker

Constituency worker

Housing officer

Industrial relations officer

Lay church worker

Member of Parliament

Political scientist

Politician

Priest/vicar

Probation officer

Psychiatric social worker

Social worker

Town crier

Trade Union worker

Volunteer worker

Youth worker

Law and related occupations

Advocate/Barrister

Advocate'sBarrister's clerk

Court usher

Legal administrator

Legal executive

Legal secretary

Notary public

Procurator fiscal

Solicitor

Security and other protective services

Bodyguard

Coastguard

Customs and Excise officer

Fire officer

Locksmith

Police officer

Prison officer

Private investigator

Security alarm engineer

Security guard

Traffic warden

Finance and related occupations

Actuary

Accountant

Accounting technician

Bank/Building society clerk

Bank/Building society manager

Bookmaker

Fund manager

Insurance broker

Insurance loss adjustor

Insurance surveyor

Insurance underwriter

Investment analyst

Management accountant

Market analyst

Market maker

Pensions manager

Tax inspector

Stockbroker

Buying, selling and related occupations

Advertising account planner

Advertising account executive

LIST OF OCCUPATIONS

Advertising copywriter

Antiques dealer

Auctioneer

Bookseller

Butcher

Buyer

Car salesman

Cashier

Demonstrator

Estate agent

Export salesperson

Fashion model

Import/export worker

Petrol station attendant

Marketing executive

Market researcher

Publisher

Retail assistant

Retail manager

Sales representative

Stock controller

Supermarket shelf-stacker

Trading standards officer

Wholesaler

Window dresser

Sciences, mathematics and related occupations

Astrologer

Astronomer

Astrophysicist

Bacteriologist

Biochemist

Biomedical scientist

Biotechnologist

Cartographer

Computer programmer

Economist

Food technician

Forensic scientist

Geneticist

Geographer

Geologist

Geophysicist

Home economist

Laboratory technician

Metallurgist

Meteorologist

Neurobiologist

Oceanographer

Physicist

Statistician

Engineering

Aircraft maintenance engineer

Biochemical engineer

Chemical engineer

Civil engineer

Control engineer

Oil derrick man

Drainage engineer

Electronics engineer

Heating engineer

Highway engineer

Marine engineer

Mining engineer

Nuclear engineer

Offshore oil/gas drilling crew

Pipeline engineer

Structural engineer

233

Manufacturing and crafts

Baker

Blacksmith

Boat builder

Bookbinder

Cabinet maker

Carpenter

Ceramicist

Clockmaker

Coremaker

Clothing cutter

Dressmaker

Engraver

Foundry worker

Clothing machinist

Materials manager

Modelmaker

Musical instrument maker

Packaging technologist

Packer

Paint sprayer

Paper engineer

Pattern maker

Photographic technician

Printer

Printer's platemaker

Production line worker

Quality controller

Saddler

Sheet metal worker

Shoemaker

Tailor

Textile colour technologist

Toolmaker

Type compositor

Typesetter

Upholsterer

Watchmaker

Textiles weaver

Welder

Construction and related occupations

Aerial erector

Lift engineer

Architect

Naval architect

Bricklayer

Painter and decorator

Building control surveyor

Paviour

Crane driver

Plasterer

Electrician

Plumber

Estimator

Quantity surveyor

Floor layer

Roofer

Formwork erector

Scaffolder

Glazier

Stonemason

Joiner

Surveyor

Land agent

Thatcher

Land surveyor

Town planner

LIST OF OCCUPATIONS

Work with animals, plants and nature

Animal welfare inspector

Botanist

Breeder

Conservationist

Ecologist

Falconer

Farmer

Farm manager

Farm worker

Fisherman

Fish farmer

Forester

Gardener

Groom

Groundsman

Guide-dog trainer

Horticulturalist

Jockey

Kennel assistant

Landscape gardener

Lion-tamer

Market gardener

Ornithologist

Pest control officer

Riding instructor

Shepherd

Stable hand

Timber technologist

Tree surgeon

Veterinary nurse

Veterinary surgeon

Wildlife reserve manager

Zoo-keeper

Zoologist

Transport and communications

Airline pilot

Air traffic controller

Aviation ground crew

Bus driver

Chauffeur

Coach driver

Driving examiner

Driving instructor

Fork-lift truck driver

Freight forwarder

Furniture remover

HGV driver

Merchant seaman

Motor mechanic

Postal worker

Taxi driver

Telecommunications engineer

Transport manager

Warehouse worker

INDEX

abroad, working 201–8
advertisements 53–6
advertising for work 66
analysing job vacancies 77–81
anxiety, pre-interview 142–4
application forms 113–123
applications
    speculative 67–71, 120–23, 220
        example 122
    telephone 123–7
assessment, self- 10–26
card file 37
    example layout 41
career break 209
careers advisory service 64–5
compassionate leave 210
confidence 178–180
contact records 37, 41
correspondence, filing 37
covering letters 105–112, 211
    example 114
    for application forms 119–20
    presentation 104
    structure 106–112
curriculum vitae 82–105, 211
    faxing 112–13
    layout 104
    skills-orientated 93–100
        example 102–103
    spelling 100–101
    standard 84–93

    example 92, 94–5
depression 43–7
diary 36, 38–9
diet 45
disability 91
education, assessing 15–16
employers, researching 50–51
employment agencies 63, 212
employment package 172–4
filing 37–43
    applications 37–41
    correspondence 37
    research 41–3
form letters 106
handwriting 105–106
headhunters 64, 214
health 44–5
homeworking 193–200, 214
information, sources 46, 204
interests, personal 89
interviews and meetings 129–65
jobcentre 64, 214
job offers 172–77
    accepting 174
    declining 175
journals, specialist 55–6
leisure, planning for 37
letters
    accepting an offer 175
    covering 105–112
        example 114

declining a job offer 176
for application forms 119–20
form letters 106
interview follow-up 167
layout 112
presentation 105–106
structure 106–112
library services 46
meetings 50–52, 146, 149–51
mentoring 45
networking 58–61, 217
contact records 37, 41
newspapers 54–5
occupations, list of 222–37
older workers 185–92
part-time work 72, 183
personality, assessing 18–21
photographs 119
planning
job-search 27–47
equipment 29, 30–33
leisure 37
work-space 28
preparation 7–26
presentation, personal 34–5,
139–40
professional registers 66
questions
application forms 118–19
interview 156–63
candidates' 163–5
records, keeping 26, 37–43
recruitment consultants 61–3, 219
redundancy 187–89
referees 90–1, 219

rejection 169–72
research
employers 50–51
filing 37–43
market 197–99
occupations 50–51
targets for speculative
applications 67–8
residential courses 147–8
routine 33–4
salary 113, 134–5, 163
selection process 75–6
self-employment 193–200, 219
skills
analysing 18–19
assessing 12–14, 16–18
transferable 18, 89, 96–7
speculative applications 67–71,
120–23, 220
example 122
stationery 30–31
telephone applications 123–7
temporary work 72, 183
time-management 35–7
training 50, 180–81
trade magazines 55–6
unemployment, on CV 88
Voluntary Service Overseas
190, 207, 221
women returners 178–84
work experience 12–13, 87–88
working abroad 201–208

COLLINS POCKET REFERENCE

Other titles in the Pocket Reference series:

Etiquette
A practical guide to what is and what is not acceptable and
expected in modern society

Speaking in Public
A guide to speaking with confidence, whatever the occasion

Ready Reference
A fascinating source of information on measurements,
symbols, codes and abbreviations

Weddings
An invaluable guide to all wedding arrangements, from the
engagement to the honeymoon

Letter Writing
A practical guide for anyone who needs to write letters,
whether for business or pleasure

What Happened When?
Thousands of dates and events in one handy volume

Prescription Drugs
Clear explanations of prescription drugs and their actions

(All titles £4.99)